Harmony
The Art of Life

Harmony
The Art of Life

By Taoist Master
NI, HUA-CHING

The Shrine of the Eternal Breath of Tao
College of Tao and Traditional Chinese Healing
LOS ANGELES

Acknowledgement: Thanks and appreciation to Janet DeCourtney, Frank Gibson and the students in the Atlanta Center for assistance in typing, editing, proofreading and typesetting this book.

Shrine of the Eternal Breath of Tao, Malibu, California 90265
College of Tao and Traditional Chinese Healing, 117 Stonehaven Way, Los Angeles, California 90049

Library of Congress Catalog Card Number 90-61994

Library of Congress Cataloging-in-Publication Data

Ni, Hua-Ching.
Harmony : the art of life / by Ni, Hua-Ching.
p. cm.
Includes index.
ISBN 0-937064-37-8 : $14.95
1. Harmony (Philosophy) 2. Taoism. 3. Sexual ethics. 4. Conduct of life. I. Title
B105.H37N5 1991 90-61994
299'.514448--dc20 CIP

This book is dedicated to those who respect and enjoy harmony in relationship with oneself and with other people of the world.

To female readers,

According to Taoist teaching, male and female are equally important in the natural sphere. This is seen in the diagram of Tai Chi. Thus, discrimination is not practiced in our tradition. All my work is dedicated to both genders of human people.

Wherever possible, constructions using masculine pronouns to represent both sexes are avoided; where they occur, we ask your tolerance and spiritual understanding. We hope that you will take the essence of my teaching and overlook the superficiality of language. Gender discrimination is inherent in English; ancient Chinese pronouns do not have differences of gender. I wish for all of your achievement above the level of language or gender.

Thank you, H. C. Ni

Warning - Disclaimer

This book is intended to present information and techniques that have been in use throughout the orient for many years. The information offered is to the author's best knowledge and experience and is to be used by the reader(s) at their own discretion. The information and practices utilize a natural system within the body and natural spiritual response, however, there are no claims for absolute effectiveness.

Because of the sophisticated nature of life and the limited information contained within this book, it is recommended that the reader of this book also study the author's other books for further knowledge about having a healthy lifestyle and practicing energy conducting exercises.

People's lives have different conditions. People's growth has different stages. Because the background of people's development cannot be unified, no rigid or stiff practice is given that can be applied universally. Thus, it must be through the discernment of the reader that the practices are selected. The adoption and application of the material offered in this book must be your own responsibility.

The author and publisher of this book are not responsible in any manner whatsoever for any injury which may occur through following the instructions in this book.

Contents

Prelude

"Tao is the destination of all religions, while it leaves behind all religions just like the clothing of different seasons and different places. Tao is the goal of serious science, but it leaves behind all sciences as a partial and temporal description of the Integral Truth.

"The teaching of Tao includes all religious subjects, yet it is not on the same level as religions. Its breadth and depth go far beyond the limits of religion. The teaching of Tao serves people's lives like religions do, yet it transcends all religions and contains the essence of all religions.

"The teaching of Tao is not like any of the sciences. It is above the level of any single subject of science.

"The teaching of Tao is the master teaching of all. However, it does not mean the teaching relies on a master. It means the teaching of Tao is like a master key which can unlock all doors leading to the Integral Truth. It teaches or shows the truth directly. It does not stay on the emotional surface of life or remain at the level of thought or belief. Neither does it stay on the intellectual level of life, maintaining skepticism and searching endlessly. The teaching of Tao presents the core of the subtle truth and helps you to reach it yourself."

Preface

Harmony is the key element of life for each individual, society, and all of humankind. Harmony exists in the weather and climate with its changes such as wind, rain, heat and cold. Although the climate sometimes makes extreme changes, the most pleasant situation is a fine day. But it still needs to be balanced with rain.

Harmony in nature is the most nutritious and supportive condition for human life. If nature lacks harmony, humans cannot live. Volcanos, earthquakes and floods are examples of disharmonious conditions or violent changes. People cannot live in their presence. So basically, the foundation of life is harmony.

Within each human being, the best condition is harmony. Internally, an individual's emotion, organs, intellect and heart all have to find harmony with one another and with the person's life. If they find harmony, the individual will be a happy, creative person. If you do not find harmony, you not only make trouble for yourself, but anything you create might harm other people too.

There are two ways to live. One way worships harmony and concentrates on cooperation and balance. The other way worships force and concentrates on fighting and winning.

In western society, Christianity was the main cultural force. Its background was the worship of one unique conquering force, Jehovah. Jesus' teaching improved the spiritual condition of his time by directing people to look for peace. However, when Darwin wrote a book about evolution, the theory of "survival of the fittest" was exalted. Darwin's objective observation has scientific value, but some people illustrated it to be a philosophy of struggling and war. That is not objective, although it could describe a stage of life.

Look carefully and you cannot totally agree with the philosophical application of Darwin's theory by saying that there has to be combat to find the fittest for survival. For example, even if two people are fighting, and if one person's shoelace is not tied well, he has made trouble for himself. The result would be to lose the fight, because his shoes argue with him. Does that mean that he is not fit to survive because he was not smart enough to remember to tie his shoe? In a war, if two war machines are fighting, the operator of the machine with a loose or poor mechanical condition will have trouble because his machine argues with him. Thus, disharmony is expressed on his side. This does not determine survival of the fittest person, but of the fittest machine.

The interpretation of the philosophical level of Darwin's work as survival of the fittest is not suitable to apply in a developed human society as fighting. In a developed human society, the survival of the fittest does not mean fighting each other. Survival of the fittest in a modern developed country means that those who can organize themselves in peace, and in one piece, will do better than those who cannot. You yourself are unified, in a harmonious condition, not only internally, but externally too. So the fittest survives because of internal harmony. That does not mean that the fittest is the most famous or the most beautiful or the most wealthy. It means that the fittest is the most harmonious.

Harmony itself is a power. Harmony is a force. The force is not directly produced by external competition. The force is produced from inside a person or situation. Harmony can work for its own purpose, which means to achieve a goal or produce the best results to benefit all sides. The harmonious condition supports the strength of all motivations. No matter who you are, a politician, businessperson, housewife, husband, teacher, etc., if you do not have harmony within yourself and within your life, you have no power or force to carry out what you wish to do. So harmony is the foundation of everything.

The misapplication of this new philosophy of competition, the worship of might, has prevailed since the last century. Practically, it was a bad situation in the human world. It expresses the devolution of human spiritual reality instead of highly evolved spiritual reality.

In China, there are many different kinds of aboriginal people. Some of them are primitive. One group worships a kind of thing called Gu. In the middle of early summer, on what the Chinese people consider the fifth day of the fifth lunar month, the worshippers go together to a field or mountain. Each one gathers a hundred different insects, reptiles and amphibians such as lizards, snakes, frogs, scorpions, centipedes, black widow spiders, bats, etc. They put those hundred small lives in a jar or chest, and keep it in a secret place inside the house. After 49 days, they open the jar or chest, and there is only one creature left. All the others are eaten up by one. These people see this remaining creature as the King God. They think it can help their lives become prosperous or give them power over other people, and so they worship it. This Gu is a primitive magic art, usually practiced by women who wish to control their lovers. This was in the past.

The worshippers serve the Gu like a god. Every third year, the person uses the poison produced by the Gu to poison someone, usually a stranger, as an offering to the Gu. They also believe that if anybody disrespects them, at nighttime the god of the Gu will fly out and eat the heart of the disrespectful one.

In times of darkness before humans developed themselves, the process of producing each Gu by letting the 100 creatures compete in a box or jar was seen to be a miniature replica of human society. In those times, human society was even worse than the society of wolves and other fierce and cruel animals. Some areas are still this same way. It is a shame. Other people are unaware that much of humanity still lives in darkness and undevelopment, because they themselves have experienced only the peace and harmony of a developed, naturally-ordered government. Unfortunately, some worldly leaders adopt the philosophy of evil competition and the worship of might, so darkness and undevelopment still exist. Some governments go to extremes with the negative expression of "survival of the fittest."

The ancient developed ones knew the danger of raising the Gu was that, even if it was not used to harm strangers, it would harm the worshipper's family. So, they concluded, "Those who raise Gu must destroy themselves by pre-existing disharmony." Similarly, the evil political leaders of the world become the Gu on a larger scale. In our observation of history, we have seen many powerful people or powerful political leaders end this way. Those leaders were too powerful; nobody could fight them, but they came to ruin by themselves because they corrupted themselves. Those people who seek power for themselves like the Hitlers, Stalins or Chinese emperors do not know the result of their actions. All powerful people have a corrupt spot inside. That is the disease that sooner or later will spread out and be their self-destruction.

So now, people have developed enough to know the eternal truth: harmony. The benefit or profit produced by harmony lasts long and is truly enjoyable. Those who build themselves into power or take advantage of people by violence or force are short-lived and finish soon. Using force does not assure anyone's long prosperity. Only by living with the everlasting truth will a person enjoy enduring life. Only the power of harmony assures eternal life. If you are married, then harmony helps you maintain good relationships in your family. If you work for people, run a business or government, or whether you are in any big or small relationship, harmony is what assures the result of good fruit.

It is wrong to make people fear you. That kind of power always corrupts internally. If a government controls and presses other people too tightly, it damages the organic condition of society. This same law of harmony can be applied to the management of each individual life and to the management of a family by the head of the family.

Harmony is natural; it is respecting or valuing each individual part of the whole. Harmony is not an idealistic concept; it is a reality for those who work for it.

Life itself is a set of conflicts. The key to success is not to accelerate or emphasize any conflict, but to diminish the conflict. For example, when we go to the market to buy something, we contact a businessman. A businessman's position is "I have to make money from this sale." A buyer's psychology is, "I would like to buy something good but cheap." There is a middle point acceptable to both the seller and the buyer. This is called harmony. At that point, the buyer gets good merchandise cheaply, and the businessman makes money. He makes a sale, and it is a good thing that he has sold to someone. You can see the conflicting interest between both sides, but harmony brings survival and help to each of them.

The same situation occurs in the relationship between a government or political leadership and the people. If the economic or political philosophy behind a government is wrong, it brings the wrong fruit and troubled times for all people. There will be no progress made in the human social evolution by any socialist who does not truly understand the nature of human life. Socialistic promotion has a defect within itself. The worship of might really brings human society back to darkness.

This book, *Harmony Serves You*, is meant to cover all aspects of life, such as individual personal life, society, men and women working together and humankind. In ancient times, people could keep away from the influences of society. They could live alone without involvement, unlike today. Today, hardly anyone can do that because modern society requires interdependency among people, businesses, states, etc. Whatever happens to society also affects the small scale of life: the individual.

This book about harmony conjuncts with my other book, *Moonlight in the Dark Night*, which will guide you in outgrowing your emotions and reaching spiritual development. I hope both books can be useful in your life.

Ni, Hua-Ching
January 31, 1991
U.S.A.

Chapter 1

Harmony is the Core of the Universe

I
Moving Forward to Harmony

Harmony between man and woman and the parallel harmony within oneself is the practical goal of Taoist spiritual learning. People have been living in the world for many, many generations and all are deeply affected by their culture. Now, in modern times and modern society, it seems that many people do not relate to their natural identities any longer. This is because many things are more mixed than what were in the past. However, when people do not know what they are, or know their own nature, it is hard for them to pose themselves appropriately or harmoniously with others.

Harmony between a man and a woman or any two people is not something that can be required from outside or guaranteed in a contract. Harmony cannot be regulated by any external authority. Harmony between a man and a woman also does not depend on a certificate of marriage. Harmony is a spiritual matter. Harmony is getting along happily. It can happen when two people become mature through understanding themselves and thus can understand each other and gracefully handle everyday situations.

It is the Taoists' understanding that harmony is a spiritual matter because it relates to each individual's personal sensitivity and the sensitivity of each situation of daily life. For example, although words may be present, communication between two people happens spiritually, through energy communication. Thus, basically, harmony comes from understanding yourself: your own mind and how you use it, your body and how it works, and your energy and what you do with it.

So we recognize the importance of harmony. We need to improve the harmony within and outside of our lives. There are people who are confused about themselves and what energy they possess. If we do not accept ourselves as man or woman, and the natural roles that we can best perform, then how can there be harmony with ourselves? I am not saying that a man has to perform a certain predefined role or a woman has to perform a certain predefined role. I am saying that each man and each woman has to find out for themselves at what kind of role they do the best. This kind of self-knowledge and clarity brings harmony. Once there is confusion, no healthy mental attitude can be produced and harmony with others becomes difficult.

Harmony comes from clarity. Harmony is achievement. It is a spiritual achievement. Harmony is generated from the spiritual growth that comes from understanding our own energy within the cooperative teamwork of the life of a family or society. Once we lose our ability to see our natural capability clearly, then harmony can never be truthfully attained.

Social scientists have their own perspective regarding men and women and their relationships in modern times. I also appreciate the ancient view of relationships described in the natural model of man and woman taken from the *Book of Changes and the Unchanging Truth* (also called the *I Ching)*, which was the spiritual perception over 6,000 years ago. At that time, there were not as many conceptual creations to confuse our vision. So from the *Book of Changes*, we might gain a different understanding of our natural potential.

There are sixty-four hexagrams in the *Book of Changes*, or *I Ching*. The first two are called Chyan and K'un. In a relationship, Chyan means the natural yang energy which in the *Book of Changes* would be illustrated by man, and K'un, the natural yin energy, would be illustrated by woman. Those hexagrams represent masculine and feminine energy in nature in the broad sense and not just with regard to people. Therefore, Chyan also means sky or the spiritual and K'un also means earth, or the physical. Thus, these hexagrams describe two types of basic energies as masculine energy and feminine energy.

A relationship between the two types of energy is just like the Tai Chi diagram, ☯ which has two equal sides, each side taking on the specific expression of either yin or yang according to its nature. However, each individual in a relationship also has two equal but opposing energies, just as presented by the Tai Chi diagram (symbol). Thus, each person also contains the creative and receptive attributes of both yin and yang. From having both attributes within yourself, you can learn to understand your own role in any relationship and perform your functions or tasks of harmonization accordingly within and without. You can also understand the value of the other person in the relationship and therefore be supportive of the other person's functions.

The *I Ching* presents an ideal model of the two genders, but keep in mind that there is always a range of variation. We have no need to make rigid typologies as in ordinary abstract discourse. The ancient women cooked, were housekeepers, child-raisers and so forth, while men hunted, fought, chopped firewood, and so forth. Now that way of life has changed. In reality, there are different types of men and different types of women; they can each do something that they are fit to do. However, let us talk about the relationship between the two energies in a traditional male/female relationship so that we can understand the ancient example of harmonization. Let us first discuss the ancient society and the evolution of the relationship between man and woman, or yang and yin. Then let us review the description of the two prime energies, the two main forces in nature. This is how we can further our discussion.

II
Unity is the Center of Life

In ancient society, at the beginning of human development, the division or distinction between the functions of male and female in daily life was not clearly divided. They did what they just did without conceptual discrimination. It means there was not the distinct division of what man ought to do and what woman ought to do. But in one stage of human development, perhaps during the last 3,000 years, the division between the function of men and women seemed to separate, until about the last 30 years or so. During this 3,000 years, most women took care of the home and children and most men provided material support for the family. If society had stayed still and modern society not evolved from that kind of situation, there would be no conflict or lack of understanding regarding the position of man and woman. However, change always occurs. Human society has become much more complicated. To provide material support for a family has become a complicated matter. It connects with the type of society and the different way of making a living. The fundamental goal of commerce is still to support life, but the means of earning that financial strength is much more complicated. The ancient hunters have changed into businesspeople.

Today, businesspeople need to understand not only the business that they are in, but also understand the domestic and world market, the political climate, military strategy, world monetary systems, the stock market, the current situation of a region and the world, accounting, taxation, banking or financing, etc. It is no longer a matter of "I carry my spear and I go to a wild field to bring back a deer or a rabbit." When this function of man changed, it forced woman to come to assist man in doing a task which the man can never accomplish by himself. At the very least, at the beginning, a businessman needs a woman at the side to help. Usually what happens is that the woman takes on a great deal of work and responsibility, and there is still more to be done. The man cannot marry multiple women, so he needs to hire other women or men as employees. Therefore, the society totally comes back to the stage of the beginning, where man and woman work together to provide the support for life in an undefined way. It was natural development; nobody organized it to become that way.

In ancient times, the hand of one man - a farmer - could produce enough to provide for his family from his field. If a man was very diligent and it was a good year, he also had something extra to show for his work. That was all the income that was available at that time. However, he needed to work from the very early morning until the late afternoon to have enough to provide for the family. If the family had male children, they would go to the fields with the father to work at a very young age, and slowly begin to learn the father's agricultural trade. The mother stayed at home with the daughters, and they not only cooked, but also preserved food, made shoes, wove fabric, sewed clothing, did laundry, fed the livestock, and many other things. Both men and women were occupied all the time just to provide for their lives. At that time, there were few criminals because everybody was so busy working for their own survival.

During that time, people primarily earned their living from nature in farming or ranching. They had a close relationship with nature. In making a living today, nature is of second importance to life. Now people make a living from other people. This coincides with the invention of the monetary system. All of this has changed how people relate to each other and to themselves. A modern farmer can produce more than enough for a whole town but needs to pay for specialized machinery to be able to do that. City people, instead of watching nature first-hand, watch it on TV. The commercial culture has promoted world confusion with all the polluted advertisements. For example, when marketing products for men, commercials on TV or in magazine ads stimulate men's desire for the product by putting a beautiful and well paid woman next to it. So if a man already eats well and dresses warmly, the commercial will stimulate him to do two things: buy the product and to think about having sex.

At this time (January 1991) I saw some statistics that indicated that 50% of women are raped or forced to have sex. It is the bad fruit of this culture. This did not happen in ancient times. Let me describe the ancient type of society. I have some knowledge of the old society of China before the communist revolution and subsequent 40 years of communist rule and I was in Taiwan for 27 years before I left the society of old China. Taiwan was also a traditional type of society. I came to the United States in 1976.

In the Chinese region of the world, the main population is the Han people. In the society of the Han people, women are protected. When I was growing up, the core or main job of women was still to take care of family life. Men worked outside the house and women worked inside. Thus, people's roles were simply defined.

The following story has been called fascinating and thought-provoking. In reading this story, some of you may make implications about it which I do not intend you to make. I want women who have been hurt by such inconsiderate behavior and suffering from the humiliation of attack to diminish their thoughts about the trouble they have had. I do not exalt this story, but only wish you to consider that customs are not the same in all parts of the world.

I would also like to describe to you the customs of a tribe called the Miao tribe who lived in the middle of western China. They were farmers and they mostly worked in the mountains. About the relationship between men and women, the good, healthy side is that they danced under moonlight, and they sang to each other. Thus a man and woman could be attracted to become lovers by singing songs and dancing. They just danced into the trees, and love happened. I think that is a healthy way for two people to pair up.

The men worked on the mountain, and the women worked there too. The unhealthy behavior was that men seem more impulsive when their sexual energy bothers them, and once they saw a woman, they would chase her. This did not happen every day. It seldom happened, but when it did happen, the woman would run away. Sometimes the man ran faster than the woman; if that was the case, the woman would lie down on the ground, and using her skirt to cover her face, she would just let the man do it. After the act was performed, the man had to go and then the woman also got up and left. She took this as a natural accident and it was not a big deal. However, it was a custom or an unwritten rule that if the man lifted the skirt to see the face of the woman, the woman would also see him and she would go back to tell the family or the village people about the man who raped her. Then the people killed the man without mercy. So, the woman's skirt originally covered her lower part but then it covered her face, and after this happened, both she and the man forgot about it. It was like one animal chasing another animal. However, if the act became involved with emotion, such as how young, how beautiful, or whose daughter or son, then evil was involved. It was not natural desire anymore, so killing happened.

I do not promote this custom. I am only telling you that during that time, such an event was not a big matter. Why did this happen so infrequently in that ancient society? Because everybody was so busy; everybody needed to work to support family life. This something only usually happened among teenagers. The man would see a shadow of a woman coming along; it could be any woman from the tribe, even the older ones. But it was not serious sex, it was a kind of animal impulse. The woman did not lose her dignity or have a psychological problem from it, because she covered her face. In other words, losing one's dignity or feeling shame is cultural. What causes a person to feel shame in one country may be something that gives a person dignity in another country. The same is true of psychological response; it is culture that determines the reaction. In that particular place, the cultural response to the event was that it was not a big deal, although of course response to anything varies from individual to individual.

In other regions, a different tribe, the people worked in the mountains. Courtship and mating was simple. There was communication and flirtation between men and women who saw each other from a distance by singing songs back and forth. To sing to each other in the mountains would be their first greeting. Later, they would ask each other questions. There would be encouragement from man's side, and refusal from the woman's side. All the while, the man would try again and again to make the woman accept him by continuing to sing songs. They would begin to approach each other, coming closer and closer, then sex would happen under a romantic atmosphere. That was a socially agreeable system of the south and southwest region of China, in mountain countries like Kwangtung and Kwang Su provinces.

I do not think that our society should try to go back to that type of original simple society. Truthfully, it cannot exist any longer. But now I am going to talk about something more complicated in today's life situation; the relationship between men and women. I wish to do a good job to help those around me, those who accept me as having something to teach them.

It is interesting to look at the whole historical situation of change in the relationship between man and woman. At the beginning, man and woman worked together. Then, when agriculture was developed, because the farmers needed to work on the land, somebody needed to cook and do all the house chores. Thus, a natural division of work occurred. In the 1990's, a woman does not need to weave fabric, make shoes, sew clothes, cook all food from scratch or feed the pigs and chickens. So naturally, this division of work is finished.

Now, through coeducation, men and women grow up almost the same. The education given to man is similar to the education given to woman. However, the sexual difference still exists. Because almost everything else but that is standardized, trouble between the sexes does not exist so much in other aspects besides the realm of sexuality. The other aspects of life which were previously impractical or prohibited can be adopted by women through some effort. Those things are much easier to harmonize with than the sexual aspect of life. So it is unavoidable that this book talks about the sexual problem or sexual topics.

The question we talk about seems like new, but it is actually not new, it is old. Suggestions and answers to questions will be seen in later chapters. So we can look for what ancient people recognized as the difference between man and woman and their positions in the natural sphere or in the universe.

The thoughts in the *I Ching* about men and women were drawn before the different aspects about their relationships became seriously conflicting in modern times. The *I Ching* gives the point of view of the ancient people. They thought that man and woman, and the masculine and feminine energies of the universe, must work together. They believed that the universe not only had the two types of energies which responded to each other, but also had countless changes of phenomenon which consisted of varying structures of the two energies. They decided to use special terms called yin and yang to describe the two different types of function or two types of force or energy. For example, their simple minds viewed the difference between the sky energy and the earth energy, brightness and darkness, strong and weak, hard and soft, male and female. They noticed that things always arose together in pairs. If there is yin, there must be yang. If there is yang, there must be yin.

Although yin and yang can be understood as two distinct and separate energies, this only happens on the intellectual level, because the two arise together. One cannot exist without the other. Because all things on this plane of existence arise as paired differences, to have just one energy could not exist. Only when the two come together can either of them be known.

Yin and yang constantly interface. Yin contracts and yang expands. Yin withdraws and yang marches forward. Yin is apparent and stagnant; yang is hidden and active. They must work together or act together. However, although yin and yang arise at the same time, they can never be totally unified. With their opposing functions, they accomplish each other. Thus, when yin grows, yang will decrease. When yang increases, yin decreases. The increasing and decreasing of two sides creates a cyclic movement. This cycle describes the interrelation and interweaving of one yin energy and one yang energy. In another sense, when the positive gets stronger, the negative gets stronger too. This principle of the paired existence of yin and yang is the law of nature and is the discovery of the *Book of Changes and the Unchanging Truth.*

From the understanding of the paired different nature of yin and yang, you know the interplay of the two types of energy is the gate through which comes the universe.

The *I Ching* describes the ideal manifestation of yang energy with the hexagram Chyan and the ideal manifestation of yin energy with the hexagram K'un. The two energies complete or complement each other. In the human sphere, we can describe this complementary relationship using yin as female and yang as male.

Please understand that this is not a rigid classification. It is a description of a relative situation, or a description of energy. It is not to say that all women have the characteristics of being feminine, passive or negative. It is also not to say that all men have the characteristics of being masculine, active or positive. Sometimes women also have man energy. Some individuals are complete because they have both types of energy. These people are usually more balanced, and do better in their lives. Sometimes an individual contains more of one type of energy than the other. What kind of energy manifests for a certain person does not depend upon physical, sexual or gender differences. It depends upon the energy differences of the people.

But let us continue our talk, not on the level of individual people, but on the level of energy. Both energies, if they work together, can accomplish each other. If both energies were to stay far apart, then nothing in the universe could be created or made productive. In work, for example, you need two types of energy to join together. This does not necessarily mean that it is a man and a woman who have to work together. It only describes the energy of two individuals.

You know, if you rigidly think that yang must be man, and yin must be woman, then your thoughts will cause trouble. In truth, men can hold feminine energy and women can hold masculine energy. A typical woman needs to exercise her creative energy and a typical man needs to have receptive energy. This is what is called "there is yin in yang and there is yang in yin."

So the *Book of Changes and the Unchanging Truth* uses Chyan to describe yang energy and K'un to describe yin energy. Chyan is strong and forwarding. K'un is compliant and peaceful. In any given situation, if the two energies are balanced one to the other, a positive condition will result. However, if there is an imbalance in the amount of either yin or yang, usually a negative condition will result.

Confucius' commented in a definite way about the two main energies of nature and human society. He was the one who was idealistic in fossilizing the teaching of the *I Ching*. He rigidly interpreted Yang as man and yin as woman. He did not understand that what the *I Ching* discussed is on the energy level or energy differences, and interrelation and their interdependence.

III
Harmony Performs Miracles

Harmony involves having two different things looking for the point at which they can link together. The point of linkage, if healthy and helpful, brings harmony. Thus, harmony is the something between two different forces. When these two forces are related or interrelated to each other, in a condition of productivity, creativity and accomplishment, that is called harmony. Above all, this type of relationship is also enjoyable. Not only is it enjoyable, but it also produces mutual support and mutual benefit for both people.

If a relationship lacks the elements as I described, there is no harmony, there is disharmony.

What I am talking about now is not an external force that brings two different forces together such as social customs, rules and laws. An internal reality or an internal need within each person or force is what brings the two forces together and ties them in union. The situation of being together is necessary; it is natural, it is not unnatural. It does not happen because another bigger or more imposing force put two different things together. Two things stay together by their own attraction towards each other, not the imposition of a strong manipulating force.

In discussing this, we need to look at the past. Let us examine the original human past, before written history, during the period of written history, and today. When we understand the experience and learning that came from the human past, we will be better able to organize our lives today.

I would like to offer you some of the reality of China's history, because China was a unique society. It has a longer history than most other countries, which means more experience and thus more wisdom. When we talk about human matters, if you have more information from a wider, deeper background, then you can have more potential for self-expansion and greater understanding. Thus, your vision will not only be limited to one spot or limited information. This is why I so readily talk about the human experience in China. Please allow me to switch back and forth from talking about human experience to talking about the *I Ching* and vise versa. By the illustration of each, I would like to show something behind them.

Let us look at the *I Ching.* The spirit of the *I Ching* was to know the secrets of the universe beyond what we can see with our eyes. The *I Ching* helps us learn what is behind nature. The universe is physical but in addition, there is something else that is not physical.

We know that all physical things change. Earth itself keep reshaping; there are volcanoes and earthquakes. The sky keeps changing in weather patterns and the stars change too. But that takes a longer time than a human lifetime. Some changes are observable, but some things cannot be observed by the short span of a human lifetime. Fortunately, we have a past record and oral passage among teachers and students which lets us know about many of the larger scale changes. The accumulation of knowledge and experience in the written records will help us understand more than only looking at our one spot of present time.

You know, the human soul is immortal. Physically, people die. When the spirit returns to human life and is newly fleshed in the new life, some memory can be regained about past learning and knowledge accumulation, past development, past achievement and past experience. So, a person's knowledge is not the limited information of today. Good knowledge must come from long observation and spiritual experience. The combination of long observation and spiritual experience can produce useful knowledge. The *I Ching* was a response to the exploration of human spirits for the deep nature.

The material comprising the written explanation of the *I Ching*'s hexagrams came to Wen Wang (that was King Wen, who was active around 1104 B.C.), and especially to one of his sons, Chuo Kong Dann (also active around 1104 B.C.). Then the *I Ching* came into Confucius' hands. Unfortunately, Confucius fossilized the teachings. He made them rigid and stiffened. Today, more than fifty percent of the written version of the *I Ching* was Confucius' work. The fault of

Confucius was to assign human roles to the hexagrams, thus creating differences of position and authority.

Confucius interpreted yin and yang as Heaven and earth. He said that Heaven, or sky, is yang and is above, and that earth is yin and is below. Then he took that framework and used it to establish the authority of the king, the authority of the father and the authority of the husband. He said that the king, emperor, father and husband were Heaven. The minister, son, daughter and wife were earth. Heaven was high above and earth was down below. Whoever was down below should always follow what is high and serve the high. The one below must bow to the high and must obey what was on high. When this "doctrine" of Confucius became overestablished, a lot of trouble began, because the authority of such positions was abused.

Even before Confucius, these beliefs were pretty much established as the convention in Chinese society in different regions. However, Confucius wrote it down according to his own narrow conception. It is a kind of misinterpretation of the universal spiritual order. So in Confucius' model of human life, the king, father or husband had the full authority over what was beneath him. This established a man-centered society.

Now let me tell you about the extremity and abuse that occurred as a result of this understanding or mis-understanding. It was an iron rule of ancient conventional society that when the king decided that the minister should die, the minister must die; he could not disobey. When the father decided that the son should die, the son must die; he could not disobey. Confucius supported this kind of social order by his writing.

So Confucius promoted the relationship between yang and yin according to his interpretation of them as Heaven and earth. One is master and one is follower. The follower must obey the master. Why did Confucius have those thoughts? Why did he write such a thing? It was because Confucius' ambition was to restore order to society and end the social turmoil that occurred at the end of the Chou dynasty. At that time, none of the feudal kings respected the central government, which was headed by the emperor of Chou. So Confucius produced his writing and teaching. His work produced a long influence over the Chinese people and was applied incorrectly to different times. It was to improve the social order and end anarchy that Confucius said that someone in the position of minister, son or wife had to obey Heaven, who in all cases was one man who was above them. In other words, you must obey your king, your father or your husband, who is always right. You must offer your obedience with no second thought in your mind.

Confucius' profession was a ceremonial master. He liked to put everything into a ceremonial style. In a conducting a social group, you need some kind of ceremonial process, but that is not the essence of life. Ceremony is not a Taoist's ultimate interest. On the level of social interaction, a Taoist has advising spirits, not spirits of ceremony or religion. They are different. The greater value of the advising spirits is objectivity while the ceremonial spirits are fixed or rigid.

The spirits of ceremonial and religious ritualism were Confucius' focus. He thought they were a help in establishing the order of society. He put all his life energy into working in that direction. However, the true spirit of an orderly society is damaged by over-emphasis upon surface concerns.

The *I Ching* is the source of ancient culture. Its interpretation by the Taoists and Confucius is totally different. The teaching of Tao does <u>not</u> talk about being in a position such as Heaven or man to produce authority and thus control the lives of others. Nor does being in the position of earth or woman mean to become passive, dependant or helpless. Rather, the position of Heaven or man is what produces service and help for the lives of others. The position of earth or woman also produces service and help for the lives of others. All positions, whether Heaven or earth, produce obligation.

Let us compare the two points of view. The Confucian interpretation is that the king is the sky or Heaven. These words are all ancient terminology for yang. In Taoism, we do not disagree with that, but to a Taoist, a high position does not mean that you have authority over everybody.

Having a high position means a bigger, wider scope; you need to take care of more people and give service on a wider scale. That is your obligation. For example, a king has a big group of people in his territory. Whatever is within his territory is the object of his service. As another example, if a father has a number of sons and daughters, he needs to take care of all of them. That is the obligation or service that comes with being the father. As for a husband, at that time on earth, the population was small. In order to help increase the human population at that time, each man had lots of women. There were many more women than men at the beginning and also, women were physically not as strong as men. So they gathered together in small communities, with the man as the center or head surrounded by a group usually composed of women. You know that in such a case, it is not easy to be the sky. The sky needs to take care of, to shade, all the women.

The Taoist spirit is totally different from the ceremonial spirit of Confucius. Taoism says that the relationship between minister and king, son and father, wife and husband, is a relationship of interdependency for natural reasons. In other words, it means the king also serves the minister and the minister serves the king. This means that a king can be a minister and a minister can be a king. The father serves the sons and daughters, and the sons and daughters serve the father. Also the husband serves the wife and the wife serves the husband. The husband serves as wife, and the wife serves as husband. There is no distinct line that determines who does what.

But Confucius drew a clear but artificial line, telling about the authority and duty of each side of a relationship. That teaching degenerated Chinese society.

My friends and readers, no matter young or old, you have some life experience. You may be married or single. You may work a job, or you may be the boss. We know one reality; if you are a husband or wife, sometimes the husband needs to be wife and sometimes the wife needs to be husband. Sometimes the general worker needs to be boss and sometimes the boss needs to do the tasks of the worker. What is done is determined by the need of the circumstance.

There is no definite line existing that rigidly describes the duties of each. For the purpose of survival and for the purpose of achievement, each person does his or her best to accomplish a common goal.

A family is a small society. A work group is also a small society. A kingdom with ministers is a big society. No matter what type of society, what is important is the relationship between the members. Each person is in a different position divided according to duty. Duty also produces certain authority, but it is an authority to carry out or fulfill the duty. It means, according to the duties accomplished, that duty carries with it a certain authority. However, authority is never absolute. It is not absolute authority over other people's life and death.

For example, the ancient division of work in a marital relationship was that the woman's work was inside the house: kitchen work, house chores, cleaning, taking care of children, etc. The man went out to the field or market, or accomplished business. Then he came back to be served by the woman. Okay, you are the man with Taoist spirit and you come home. You see that your wife is really busy and the house is not clean enough. The children are crying and here and there are some things your woman's hand cannot touch all the time. At this time, you, the husband, can also do the inside work of the house. Why not? Conversely, when there are few children or they have grown up and moved out, when everything is neat inside the house, and the husband needs help with his outside job, the wife can help. There is no way to say the wife should not help the husband or the husband should not help the wife.

If you are a Confucianist, you would draw a firm line between what the husband should do, and what the wife should do. You think that a man is superior and a woman is inferior. Housework is inferior, and a man should not touch it. Confucius produced myriad hardships for being a woman and a wife. That is the misinterpretation of yin and yang that started from the *I Ching.*

The *I Ching* came to the hand of the son of King Wen, Chou Kong Dann. He assisted his brother King Wu (reign 1122-1115 B. C.) who had just assumed his father's throne.

The *I Ching* became a political tool to support the newly established dynasty. At the end of the Chou Dynasty, which was 500 years after the death of King Wen, society become disordered again. At that time, Confucius was a scholar and a discharged prime minister to the feudal prince of Lu (now Shang Tung province, which is Confucius' hometown). He was quite active in his attempt to reorder society near the end of the Chun Dynasty. Confucius admired Chou Kong Dann's work on the *I Ching* and wished to use the *I Ching* to return order to society. However, this was a time when might was right and Confucius' plan did not work. He extended his rigid interpretation, but he did not see that this would have a long negative influence on society, because it made society inflexible. This was not his expectation.

In Taoist philosophy, the sky can be earth, and earth can be sky. You can see that in the first and second chapter in the *Tao Teh Ching*, where Lao Tzu says that Tao is universal orderly spirit or spirit of universal order, it can not be defined rigidly. If defined rigidly, it can no longer be the universal orderly spirit. Lao Tzu's work can be considered a spiritual response to the degenerate society of China.

In the second chapter of the *Tao Teh Ching*, Lao Tzu says that high and low, yin and yang, front and rear, being and nonbeing, etc. are paired forces. Each of the two different forces help, accomplish and complement each other. The two differences do not express fighting. The two different forces, in reality, are interdependent, and work together for mutual help. It is out of interrelated need. That is called universal orderly spirits. It is not that you decide what ceremony should be done, who should bow and when they should bow, how many bows, etc. For a minister to need to kneel down when he sees his king, and to be able to offer only obedience and never to disobey is totally different from the advisor spirits of Taoism. What Taoism offers to society is to be objective, rather than subjective.

When facing uncertainty, the wise advice is to be objective. It is not because you are king, father and husband that you must be wise or wiser than your minister, wife or children. Just the fact that you are in a certain position does not mean that you have wisdom. Wisdom is something you must constantly reach for as you endeavor to carry out your duty. Only wisdom should be followed, not just an order. When you face uncertainty in making big decisions, and when your intellectual accumulation of information fails to decide what needs to be done, the next step is to use the *I Ching*.

In ancient times, the heads of state did not depend on one person alone to make decisions. Six people were chosen. They had to fast for hours or days in order to dissolve their internal confusion and purify the mind and body. Then each person would make the divination. At least two systems of divination were used, one of them being the *I Ching*. Because each person's position and subconscious background are different, the answer received by each person from the divination was also different. The leader observed each person's result. Each person offered a new thought or a new light to shine upon a new direction. The purpose was not for the leader to decide whose divination was best or most correct, but to get six different objective points of view about a situation. Then the leader could apply more thinking and do more homework before making an important decision. The practice of six people helping to make one decision is not what I recommend. But I do recommend that you study the *I Ching* and learn the principle of balance and objectivity in making a decision.

Disharmony or conflict is unnatural. It creates an unhealthy situation. Instead, in a natural, healthy, organic situation, man can help woman and woman can help man; woman can act as man, doing what man does and man also can act as woman, doing what woman does. They need to help each other. This is a Taoist illustration.

The purpose of our discussing this is not for me to ask you to study Confucius' teachings, nor for me to ask you to study Taoism. I offer this illustration to help you know what can serve you, and what does not serve you, in your life.

IV
More Harmony, Less Disputes

During the last 2,500 years, Confucius' elucidation of the natural orderly society in the *I Ching* was used. It describes the emperor being of Heaven, and the ministers and people being of earth. Similarly, a father is Heaven or sky to all members of the family, just as a husband is Heaven to his wife. The emperors used Confucius' teaching to control their empire. The fathers, as head of the families, also used his teachings to rule the household and control women. If the emperor or father was wise, Confucius' teaching found right application. If the emperor or father was unwise, then Confucius' teaching supported his unwise leadership and mis-management. Thus, Confucius' teaching is circumstantial, like the teaching of all religions. Even in today's China, the stiffness and rigidity of society brought about by Confucius' teaching has not improved much. He was credited for holding societies and families together when things were normal. But the worst thing is that his teaching also supported dictatorships and unwise men at the times when things went wrong.

No sage offers a teaching applicable to all times. All teaching needs to be updated, not only that of Confucius, but also of the other sages, Sakyamuni, Mohammed, Jesus, Moses, (except Lao Tzu, who did not advise people to hold onto anything as the final truth). Even Tao is a reluctant term for truth. It seems that nobody should hold the dead body of a sage as the living truth of all time. Otherwise, those teachings only bring more harm than benefit.

V
Harmony is the Cornerstone of a Happy Life

In life, you must attain harmony with some person in a relationship, if not all people. You also must attain yourself. Harmony within yourself is spirituality. Many people have a gross misconception: they think that going to church or going to worship is a spiritual obligation or a good spiritual deed. It is not; going to church is a cultural custom.

Spirituality is so intimately and significantly connected with each individual life that it cannot be considered as a series of singular events such as going to church each Sunday. The reality of true spirituality is internal harmony. Although internal harmony involves the physical, emotional, mental and spiritual levels, it can be attained by spiritual growth and the understanding of your own spiritual nature. Without spiritual growth and understanding, there is no harmony among the different concepts in your mind. Without such growth and understanding, there is no way to reconcile the different approaches of the two sides of the brain. Spiritual harmony manifests the unity above the relative reality of the application of our minds in general circumstances.

Even if we are concerned with the physical and emotional levels, the main key is still the spiritual harmony within us. This is important. However, harmony is a fruit of spiritual development. There is no "forever" harmony, there is "forever" work of internal and external attunement and adjustment.

Let us also talk about external harmony so as to give light to help us consider all matters of spirit. The same principles that we learn externally can be applied to internal harmony. Spiritual growth and harmony are not fantasy; they are not high ambitions. They are necessities for a good and complete life. Spiritual harmony with your partner and spiritual harmony within yourself are necessities that support your health and well being.

When people are in the normal condition of their lives, they usually do not notice their own internal disharmonies. In general, people experience them on some occasions or circumstances, over relatively simple matters, when they find it difficult to make decisions. Or they find that they are facing an event with an anxious psychological attitude within, amounting to a crisis. The disharmony of the inner being brings us to the verge of sickness. It can cause something as serious as collapse, but an ordinary sickness can find its remedy by self-improvement. However, do not wait until that moment. It is important to attain harmony in each minute of each day's life, within each contact, within each relationship and each kind of business transaction.

VI
Harmony Rewards All People

The universe developed from formless energy. It formed itself through a process of change.

First came the formless energy, then the energy changed itself to become traceable. Thus, in formless energy, there comes the traceable energy and untraceable energy. Traceable energy is close to the material sphere of existence but it is still not totally material. That is chi. The untraceable energy is close to the spiritual sphere of existence but it is still not totally spiritual.

The Universal Father is the untraceable but forming energy. It became the first being of the universe. Thus, it is called God.

The Universal Mother is the origin of the untraceable formless energy. It is called Tao.

In spiritual development, we know that the world and each human being changed from non-beingness to become beingness, from nothingness to become something. So nothingness or non-beingness is the mother of beingness and somethingness. We call that nothingness or non-beingness the Universal Mother. If the Universal Mother stayed formless, with nothingness and non-beingness, then there would be no universe.

Let us view the Universal Mother. The Universal Mother comes from the interplay of formless and form, nothingness and something, non-beingness and being. The Universal Mother is the origin of the formless and the formed. She is nothingness or non-being. Thus, she is the source of all things and all being. Thus, the entirety of the universe is the Universal Mother.

The new sphere of the formed world is a late arrival. That is what you call the physical world. The world brings the duality between the physical sphere and the mind. The development of mind sees the offerings of the Universal Mother, thus it comes to know there is a Universal Mother.

I have never seen your mother or father. However, by knowing you, I know you must come from a father and mother. You know that I also must have had a father and mother. By knowing the descendants or offspring, you know the existence of the common source or Universal Mother. In spiritual learning, once you know the mother which is the essence of the universe, you need to forsake the ramifications of the offspring, but keep your spirit together with the universal source. Keep to the mother, where all lives, all beingness and all things are produced. It is a spiritual practice to keep to the spiritual root. That is the key of spiritual practice.

So our being goes from non-being to being, from shapeless spiritual energy to become a form with physical energy. Behind physical energy is our soul, the shapeless spiritual energy. We know that our life is the offspring of the formless origin or formless mother. The formless origin is so important that all religions developed spiritual practices to keep one embracing the origin, the mother or one's own pure spirit, before it became formed as something else.

It is truthful and undeniable that all beings and things come from non-being and nothingness. Human people, once they come to being, can learn that their background comes from non-being. Human beings can follow the universal subtle origin by continuing its productivity and bringing something into the world spiritually or physically.

First level spiritual learners like to have some formed thing in front of them to help them gather spiritual energy. If anything can help people gather their spiritual focus, that must be a form. A form can be a picture or image, a precious stone, a cross, prayer beads, etc.; they are external messenger of the formless spirit they represent. The position of mankind in nature is to first have a complete bodily form, then add to it with a developed mind which can gather spiritual energy at the higher levels to become a completely developed being.

The Universal Mother has no form. It is usually difficult for less developed minds to be with no form.

Do you still have a question about the gender of the Universal Mother, about whether she is masculine or feminine? That question cannot be answered because the Universal Mother does not have gender. The Universal Mother is universal reproductivity. It is energy.

Different religions talk about God. A beneficial form to consider as a spiritual image of God is familiar to people. Why, and how is it used? Because God is not visible, people assign various shapes or images to represent the Universal Mother. However, no matter what form they take, they all represent the Universal Mother. So, in religion, it is a spiritual practice to use form, but the images are not the final truth. They are used for human spiritual benefit.

The Universal Mother comes from the subtle level and becomes more apparent and more powerful as form is taken. The apparent level is also the level of the universal impetus. There is a process of building the universal impetus. From the vast, profound universal being or Universal Mother grows the universal impetus.

So first is universal being, then universal impetus. One thing comes to be two things. So from the first comes the second, the one brings the two. By the action of the impetus, the universal being becomes a power of reproductivity and manifestation. The Universal Mother represents natural reproductivity. The internal force of impetus brings forth the manifestation. The unmanifested sphere of the universe is the latent power of reproductivity of the universe. It is recognized as the Universal Mother.

In daily life, this means that a wise woman does not reject man. She does not reject what is masculine. Masculine represents the impetus of the universe, and the woman presents the universal being as Universal Mother. The Universal Mother cannot singly bring anything into being without splitting itself in two and combining reproductivity with impetus. So she splits herself to become two, gradually growing impetus within the universal being. In human life, it similarly takes two to accomplish reproductivity.

Thus the wise woman does not reject the other sex. She accepts and adapts to the differences. She enjoys, appreciates and uses the difference to bring about and accomplish her goal of reproductivity. That level means marriage and bringing up children, but that is the narrow sense. In a broader sense, it means developing all good things in all aspects of life.

Impetus is not outside the Universal Mother but inside. After the split occurred, the world began to have the spheres of masculine energy and feminine energy which are called yang and yin.

It is important to balance the yin and yang; it is always balanced on a universal level. These two energies are also called universal generating energy and accomplishing energy. The two energies generate each other and accomplish each other. This is why there are two sexes in the universe, not just one. Universal generating energy is the same as impetus and universal accomplishing energy is reproductivity.

Any woman who has achieved wisely enough will not reject a man in her life. Because she is Universal Mother, she holds both generating energy and accomplishing energy. If she is smart and does not scatter her energy, the impetus or generating energy builds up within herself. This impetus is transformed to be her man. This means that her energy vibration attracts a man at a similar level as the one she is on, and he comes into her life. This is a narrow explanation. The impetus energy within her being is the masculine energy in her life. This pushes her to become active, creative and initiating as a male and achieve what a man can achieve.

In any group there are leaders and followers, workers or subordinates. The universal impetus always likes to be a leader, but a leader without a subordinate, worker or helper will never accomplish anything that is really beneficial, because he is only generating energy without fulfillment. Thus, a wise woman recognizes the different sex to be important in her life. A wise woman can accept a man to initiate and be a leader in a project. This allows her to fulfill the accomplishing energy within the woman herself. A wise man can also accept a woman to initiate.

On this path of the tradition of Tao, the worship of the Universal Mother means that people do not compete to be the leader. The leader is impetus. Impetus is not more valuable than the power of reproductivity, or the workers or helpers of the impetus. Together, they accomplish a productive project.

In a man-dominated world, men usually think they are more important than women. However, men who think this are unwise. They become egotistical if they believe that they are above somebody. Practically, such men do not see that the function of yin and yang is on the energy level. It is not the physical differences between male and female, because all can do general work except giving birth to children. The male function is just natural impetus. Real accomplishment, real fruit, is brought about by the cooperative energy of the woman or feminine energy. Followers, workers, governmental ministers, subordinates or teamsters, aside from the leaders, can all be considered as the feminine or accomplishing type of energy.

This is to explain impetus and productivity on the level of energy.

This understanding is taken from the original Taoism which came from millions of years of observation of nature. Taoism itself is not observation, because observation establishes two; it is the real reflection by natural lives which could see the truth. This is more profound than any ordinary human intellectual mind can create.

VII
The Spiritual Potential of the Of Typical Yang or Masculine Energy in a Personality

The masculine energy in nature symbolizes the universal creative energy. It is the universal Yang nature, the fatherliness of nature. Great indeed is the sublimity of the generating, creative, spiritual energy to which all beings owe their beginning and which permeates all space.

The four seasons bring about the difference of natural energy as a complete natural cycle; spring is generating, summer is prospering, autumn is astringent and winter is storing. This cyclic pattern can also be applied to understand individual human life. All individual beings would be benefitted by attaining the knowledge of cyclic movement by taking the example of weather to manage their lives and flow with natural cycles of their internal and external changes. It is a man's nature to create an environment suitable for everyone to live. That is a high expression of the creative energy of a man.

The attributes of sublimity and success apply to the creative person who lives in harmony with his or her own nature. A creative individual brings creative energy into full play with a clear direction from the beginning to the end, and the individual is aware of the way in which each of the steps, as pictured by the lines in the first hexagram of the *Book of Changes*, is completed in a proper way and in its proper time. The individual mounts on this energy, forwarding the life goal undauntedly and undefeatedly like riding on a chariot driven by six dragons or like the moving cloud in the sky as described by the hexagram.

The creative movement of an individual, with its beginnings and endings, are like the hexagrams of the *I Ching*. Each hexagram is a symbolic representation of a life or event. The six lines of the hexagram express six phases or stages of an event or life. Each step or line is completed in due time. The individual takes each step as if climbing a ladder to reach the highest point by forwarding life with enduring, undaunted energy. This life force is like a cloud chariot drawn by six dragons.

The way of creative energy is through constant change and transformation. Thus, each thing receives its true nature and destiny and comes into permanent accord and harmony with great nature. Accord and harmony furthers and preserves the creative life. With each thing thus finding its mode, great and lasting harmony arises in the world. This is expressed in the concepts of the perseverance, the permanence and the integrity of Tao.

The creative power of the spiritually developed one towers high above the multitude of beings. All dominions are united in peace within this individual.

Observing the movement of Heaven which is full of power, the superior one of spiritual attainment keeps making oneself stronger and untiring.

Of all that is good, sublimity is supreme. Success is the coming together of all that is beautiful. Furtherance is the agreement of all that is just. Perseverance is the foundation of all actions of the spiritually poised person.

How great indeed is the creative one! The individual is firm and strong, moderate and correct, pure, unalloyed and spiritual. The peace and harmony of each moment are that individual's most significant creations.

Individuals of great spirit accord their character with Heaven and earth; in their light, with the sun and moon; in their constancy with the four seasons; and in the good and evil situations they face, with good spirit. They maintain themselves with clear knowledge of gods and spirits when they act in anticipation of Heaven. Heaven does not contradict the known foundation; when you follow the will of Heaven, you makes yourself as creative as Heaven.

All their lives, individuals of spiritual awakening are creatively active. This is the way they carry out undertakings. Such individuals move with the times.

VIII
The Spiritual Potential of the Typical Yin or Feminine Energy in a Personality

The feminine energy in nature symbolizes the receptive energy of the universe. It is the manifestation of the universal yin nature as the universal motherliness of nature.

Perfect indeed is the sublimity of the receptive energy. All beings owe their lives and birth to its support. It realizes the will of nature within.

The receptive energy in its richness carries all things. Its nature is in harmony with boundless tolerance. It embraces everything in its breadth and illumines everything in its greatness. Through it, all individual beings attain success.

The good fortune of peace and perseverance depends on our being in accord with the boundless nature of the earth.

The person of spiritual superiority learns from the receptive devotion of the earth to have breadth of character and carries the outer, worldly life. This is in the physical life.

With selfless purpose, all things are furthered by the feminine motherly energy. In the nature of the earth, there lies the light freely offering its cooperation to all.

Lasting perseverance furthers all lives. It ends in the great accomplishment of all great things.

The receptive is altogether yielding yet firm in its life. It is altogether still, yet in its nature uprightly furthering and forwarding.

If the feminine energy follows, it finds the correct understanding, guidance and cooperation. This is to learn and obtain that which is enduring. Nothing is more enduring than Tao. Tao has no self. It embraces everything and in its power to proceed is most subtle and light-giving.

The way of the receptive - how devoted it is! It receives Heaven into itself and acts in its own time and way.

IX
Interdependency of the Two Types of Energy in Nature

Mountain energy resembles young men or masculine energy. The mountain expresses elevation, nobility, creativeness, and pride. Lake energy symbolizes young women or feminine energy. The lake represents nourishment, support, beauty and charm. So mountain and lake are combined together in perfect and beautiful harmony.

The sun also symbolizes masculine energy. The sun's strongest time expresses the middle age of a man. His creative energy is then in peak condition. The moon symbolizes feminine energy. The autumn moon is the strongest energy in the whole year's cycle. This can be demonstrated by the ocean tides; they are strongest at this time. The energies of the sun and moon, of yin and yang harmonize beautifully. They describe the natural manly and womanly energy. It was Confucius' rigid interpretation that described the role of man and the role of woman, instead of objectively describing the model of natural man and woman.

When talking about energy and the sexes, the above sections gave the Confucian thought, thus, it always mentions men or male energy first. A woman student questioned, "Is this necessary? Women are tired of coming in second." A Taoist does not agree with Confucius' establishment that a society of men and women should be structured in a rigid way. It was written this way only to introduce the discussion. Regarding being in the first or second place, the second place is often better than first place. Being in second place often provides a position of choice, while first place is usually subjected to demands of others.

In conventional Chinese society, it is told that the custom of choosing a permanent mate was started by Fu Shi. Let us consider that human life has experienced most of its development within the last 8,000 years. The system of marriage only began 3,000 years ago. Before that time, how to choose an appropriate mate was a special knowledge or an immortal secret. It existed before the rigid marriage system.

At the beginning, the marriage system was simple. A young man only needed to bring two wild geese to the family of a young woman to decide the betrothal. At the time of the marriage, a fur or hide of animal or fish would be the gift, but that was changed by Confucius' emphasis about the rituals of marriage. According to his doctrine, first a matchmaker must be consulted. Second, the young man must give six different gifts to the woman's family. The woman's dowry was also an important issue. Under Confucius' plan, marriage was more like a business transaction made by the parents and elders of both families. It seemed not to have any concern about the bride or groom. Usually the marriage was a kind of "blind marriage" - the man and woman knew nothing about each other.

After the marriage, the position of the woman was to serve the husband and provide children. The man's position was to serve the family.

If the woman was smarter, she managed her husband. At that time, whether a couple had good fortune or bad fortune was almost totally determined by the location in which they lived, in other words, what kind of land they owned and how much the land produced. People basically lived from the land and had no other expectations. The high morality in life could be summed up easily: be diligent in work, and frugal in expense.

A woman need to make clothing and shoes for the whole family, preserve and prepare food, and also take care of a dozen chicken, a number of pigs, etc. That was the fullness of life at that time. People who lived at this time did not complain about lots of work or little land. Wealth was the natural outcome of working hard or having a lot of land. Everybody took care of their own life. Most farmers did not have servants or employees. Only in society did people hire workers. In a village or a bigger town, a better-off family might have one or two workers; that was considered to be an admirable position.

This simple way of life lasted a long time in most parts of China. The real change to this way of life began around 200 years ago, when China started to contact the rest of the world. The big wave of Western modern civilization surged upon Chinese society. Unfortunately, China did not respond well and has not been doing well since that time. China's response was influenced by Confucius' rigid social directions and the simple nature of most Chinese farmers. The nature of Chinese farmers was too simple to handle complex worldly affairs.

Realistically, Chinese people have changed since the arrival of Western influence. Although the ancient farmers were honest and earnest, their descendants are not always the same as their ancestors. They hold hostility, hatred and jealousy towards others. It was taught to them by the new social leaders. If it were not for the new social teaching, they would still be pure and simple humans.

In Chinese society, past and present governmental rulers have servants. These servants often treated people worse by using the rulers' self-established authority. It does not come from the people. Most Chinese people learned that it is their lifetime wish to never have any contact with the government or its servants. This was true in the past; certainly this has been worsened under communist rule.

Chapter 2

The Meeting of Yin and Yang: -Competition Brings Harm -Cooperation Brings Survival

For a long time our human ancestors experienced the difference between the two types of force, which we call yin and yang, in their natural environment and in themselves. They also discovered the natural cycle of energy variation, which they divided into five phases: spring, summer, autumn, winter, and the transitional phase existing between each of the four main changes. Later, they applied these five phases to a vast scope of matters and changed the names to five natural forces: wood (sprouting or generating growth), fire (full growth), metal (collecting or contracting), water (storage) and earth (harmonizing). Each of the five forces was recognized to have attributes of both yin (passive) and yang (positive) nature.

Thus, the main knowledge attained by the ancient natural mind was the difference of gender. They learned to use knowledge of the difference between masculine-type energy and feminine-type energy to classify all things in the world. The most striking development learned about the differences between the two energies was that there is a way to compose a constructive scenario rather than have the two differences fight each other.

The ancient ones also found that between the two forces, there is sometimes something higher, something neutral which is balancing energy.

Our mind was developed from the minds of our ancestors. The ancient natural knowledge is the impressed image from a long period of time of gathering common experience. It is not knowledge like modern knowledge which puts forth a supposition and establishes a test to bring about the conclusion. Natural knowledge came before the human mind developed into the modern mind. The mind is a latecomer. After people lived with their natural environment, they received growth of mind. Further, the mind developed applications that were independent from physical reality, such as abstraction, imagination, etc.

It took the mind a long time to develop enough to know the nature of the environment and the body environment, which keeps impressing the mind to reflect. By this reflection, the ancient people came to know the difference between the two types of energy, externally and internally. With this foundation of recognition, the ancient mind classified the world under two types as masculine and feminine. These two types are noticeably a generalization, and do not describe a specific individual. The ancient mind sees that masculine energy is active, aggressive and motivated, and feminine energy is receptive and passive. We consider this as merely an idea or a common concept that reflects the reality of the two genders. You do not have to use the words masculine and feminine - you can call those two energies a car and a bus or anything you want to, but the two types of energies exist.

This classification is natural, but it does not involve judgment about whether one of the energies is good or bad, beneficial or not beneficial. We need a basic structure to exercise our capability of recognition and to have a means to communicate our understanding with one another.

Yang energy can be called sun energy, and yin energy can be called moon energy. Yang energy is also called fire energy and yin energy is called water energy.

It is not proper to say "a man must be that way," or "a woman must be this way" according to the categories of yang or yin. Each individual responds with each kind of energy or a combination of both according to what is necessary for the life situation facing him or her in the moment. Thus, when the classifications of yin and yang serve as the foundation of knowledge, they are not rigid teachings which makes people act according to a set definition.

Humans developed from animals. At least, human nature in some areas is close to animal nature, especially the specific features of gender differences. Many years of observation by the ancient Taoists brought them to understand that the masculine energy of the world or in a society can be aggressive and warlike in its negative extreme. In its positive extreme, it can be active and protective. They also came to understand that the feminine energy of the world or in a society can be passive and stagnant in its negative side when it extends to the extreme. In its positive side, it can be cautious and supportive.

The ancient Taoists also discovered something in family life. It is that masculine energy extends itself to be fatherliness. The fatherly energy tends to be ruling, forcing, conquering, and imposing to its children and other members of the family. But this type of energy brings about what a man needs for himself, his family and to further the goals of a community. That expresses typical masculine nature and approach.

A typical feminine nature extends itself to be motherliness. Opposite and balancing to the masculine nature's approach in the family, the motherly approach tends to handle a situation with gentleness. Motherliness helps without attitudes of conquering, imposing or lowering. Instead, it is harmonizing. She does not achieve her goal for herself or for her family by force.

So from here, the ancient Taoists found the new strength: harmony. They established their teachings upon harmony. The teaching of Tao gains its value by teaching harmony for the spirit. A philosophical foundation, as a teaching of a spiritual school, does not express its own authority, as do monarchs, rulers, conquerors, and soldiers or any negative force which have power over others. Truthfully, harmony is the real spiritual authority which exists above general religious promotion with its spitting tendency. The teaching does not support the one-sided performance of authority. Nor does it support the one-sided performance of being overly passive and sacrificing. It teaches that a better life and a better world can be obtained by cooperation between aggressive male energy and gentle female energy. The eternal balance between the two is the law of universal nature.

The modern philosophy of competition is basically a description of the negative extreme of the masculine force. Darwin, in his theory of evolution in which he states that the fittest survive, fully recognized this. One interpretation of his theory is " When I live, you are not allowed to live, or because you die, so I live." During these last 200 years, Darwin's philosophy was exemplified by western powers who made the less industrialized nations into colonies. They colonized them by their aggressive and warlike behavior. The communist party particularly accepted that as the only truth of life. It is all proof that the philosophy of competition brought more immature behavior to the world.

All immortal souls have lived in the world and have observed it for a long time. This is the spiritual development of humans. Thus when you see Tao, you see a big tree and you also see small grass. How can you decide that the truth of life is competition?

Universal nature glows in everything. All life, if dutiful, looks for self-strengthening. Both the big tree and small grass are looking for or displaying the nature of self-strengthening. Their purpose is not to look for competition.

In today's world, people need to look for a job. They maintain a position to earn income for their survival. An employer likes to hire somebody who is intelligent, does the job, is diligent in work, trustworthy in duty, and has the skills to accomplish assignments. People of different thought would think only by going through competition, contention and fighting, conquering and winning can their survival purpose can be fulfilled. In reality, we each have to prepare ourselves with good qualities for employment or self-employment.

A healthy attitude does not include, "I need to get all the rewards from the world because I am the best. I beat all others." If you keep that type of thought in your mind, you are externally motivated. You will become what you are not because you are comparing yourself with others or imitating them. You will be pushed to become what you are not, even if you can achieve your external goal. You will not reward yourself by what you are doing.

The wisdom for living in the world is first to find what you really are, and then to refine and strengthen yourself. You are not trying to imitate others but you work with what you already have and try to improve it. Do not try to get ahead by pushing people down to raise yourself high.

Using an international example, Japan became aggressive from its singular wish to swallow China. Japan thus invaded China. That action brought about an eight-year war (1937-1945) which exhausted both nations. Japan could have accomplished her goals a different way instead of exhausting herself through aggressive and warlike behavior. If Japanese leaders had decided to take China through commerce and trade instead of by military invasion, the reward could be higher and may have belonged to both sides. Thus, Japan could have accomplished her goals by being supportive and cautious. After the war, Japan put her energy into commerce and industrial achievement, and is excelling today in world economy. Other countries like Germany and Italy, if they had put their strength into industry and commerce instead of fighting World War II, would also be a great peaceful strength.

Industry and commerce survive on the response of need. This tells that the philosophy of self-interested survival of the fittest brings more harm to the world when expressed in a negative way. We have all human history to tell you that simple fact.

When the rooster chases away the other rooster and conquers the hen, he then has to work hard to stand on top of the hen. Do you believe the rooster has more enjoyment than the hen? If human leaders have achieved higher than the rooster, it is their wisdom that has brought about all possible beautiful achievement instead of negative actions.

At any time when masculine energy dominates, the world appears too fiery. There are lots of fights and the world hardly has any peace. In some locations, not only geographically but also religiously, people are fiery. This means they tend to be militant and war-like.

Mostly, war describes the negative extreme of masculine energy. The negative extreme of feminine energy is withdrawal, hiding, refusing to face situations and refusing cooperation for useful action. Some influential leaders of the big social scale, by being overly aggressive and warlike, acted as the negative examples for human history.

I admit the nature of Taoist teaching appears to move towards feminine worship and the worship of water, but this is because of the predominance of the negative, fiery, masculine energy in the world. However, there must be a balance between fire and water. With such a balance, a cooperative world will bring about common prosperity for all people. The aggressiveness, forwardness, and expansion of yang energy alone without the conservativeness, self-control and harmonizing power of yin energy only brings disaster.

No religious teaching is higher than the teaching of harmony attained by the balance of rational and physical strength. This is done in a relationship by each individual with the effective use of both the negative and positive aspects of masculine and feminine energies. Generally, the positive aspects express themselves; the negative aspects are only used with moderation to return the positive aspects to a forward motion.

Sometimes patience is needed for the balance of the two forces to take place. This balance is what is needed for the true improvement of human life on the levels of individuals and society at large.

A piece of music with a beautiful melody is not only composed of highly pitched notes. All different strengths and pitches of sound bring about a joyful piece of music. People forget the truth in their lives when they become oriented toward one extreme side or another. That is like preferring high notes to low notes, or vice versa.

Q: When a man and a woman do not choose to be married, can they still have sexual relationship in some way?

Master Ni: Perhaps a healthy practice between a man and a woman, not rigidly or formally married, is Taoist companionship. By practicing this, each person still keeps his or her individuality; each makes spirituality the center of his or her life. Taoist companionship is sometimes better for personal growth than marriage. Both ways, when done positively, can be the same energy expression of a mutually beneficial and supportive relationship between two people. A formal marriage agreement can be just a different way to take care of social, financial and legal details for each individual. Financial and legal arrangements can be taken care of in other ways to provide support and protection of the two individuals who care about each other's lives and well-being.

In Taoist companionship, out of physical need, woman needs a "sun partner," and man needs a "moon partner." They come together maybe once a month, in engagement of energy adjustment. That means sexual attunement. The man is achieved already to have no ejaculation so no tragedy will be brought to the world or to the woman. This perhaps describes an ideal situation which is not often seen in today's society.

In general society, a person who is not formally married but has a sexual life is usually considered immoral. However, sex is not a matter of morality. If marriage is only for sex, the ceremony is unnatural already in the first place. Spiritually, sexual energy is the life energy in each individual which can be transferred to be a power. It is not to suggest that everyone should do the extreme ascetic practice; at least part of sexual energy can be transferred by higher interest and spiritual cultivation. For example, sexual energy can be transferred to be health. Health is a power, long life is a power and having a good brain is a power; all of these come from sexual energy. This is why Taoists learn to be self-controlled in the matter of sex.

Meditation is also important. When you meditate, more or less you can see yourself and understand whether you act impulsively or with self-control. Do not allow your meditation to weaken your healthy life actions. The high sensitivity that comes from meditation sometimes makes people who live a meditative life scared of everything. However, all people have to stand up clearly to cope with the necessities of life.

Through all the stages of life, there is not much that one can escape. If people could, they would probably escape from all the troubles, but this is not possible. We must cope with daily life. We spend the correct amount of time and energy we need to take care of our external needs. Then, we can enjoy our internals with no interference, but this happens only when we handle the externals well. That is achievement.

If you are not achieved, you are psychologically weak. In each moment, if each thought you think is not for yourself, then it is for trouble, and you live for trouble. If you spend time thinking about the troubled, built-up world rather than your own good life, you are a person who lives for the sake of trouble.

Q: It is not only hard to find a good man, it is also hard to maintain a good relationship. People break up so often now.

Master Ni: In the sphere of male/female relationships, this is my advice:

Not too long ago I moved onto some mountain land. The land was rough, so I needed to hire someone to help me flatten part of it. One man who helped me with some backhoe work was about 38 years old. He had been married and had a nine-year-old son; there was a divorce, and his ex-wife and son went to live in another state. He met someone new and remarried, but after several months, they divorced.

Recently, he came over to help me with a certain job, and brought his new girlfriend with him. The three of us walked together on the land to discuss the area that needed work. The woman was about 29 years old. She also knew how to work with a backhoe, and she played the harp as a hobby.

This is what I mentioned to the man and woman. I said, if you are interested in having a relationship, it is not like the work you do with a backhoe; it is much more delicate. It is similar to playing a harp; if the strings are not tuned, the music sounds awful. Once the instrument is tuned with the skill of a trained hand, beautiful music is heard. A relationship is just like that, but the strings that need to be tuned are yourselves. You need to attune yourselves, because there is no ideal man for a woman, and there is no ideal woman for a man.

People come together when they feel interested in each other. The best foundation for a good relationship is a mutual interest in some work that can be done together. A shared interest, such as giving a certain type of service to the world or running a business, can help two people come together.

In most relationships, unless there is an actively shared interest that involves a lot of each person's energy, any small conflict can make one or both partners lose patience and go. This is why the Tradition of Tao recommends a life of service to others. It can be a uniting focus for a couple. A sweet and rewarding life of service through charity or business can be supported by a good relationship. Everybody needs to work hard to earn a living. It is a sweet feeling for each member of a couple to help each other. A real spiritual relationship cannot be achieved by jumping from one person to another, then again to another.

You can learn how to have a good relationship in a process similar to learning how to play the harp to produce good music. No one was born a naturally good wife or good husband, or a perfect boyfriend or girlfriend. It is your effort that makes you become appreciated by your partner. If you do not like to make that effort, then you will jump from one relationship to another, and it will never end. There is fun, but there is never any psychological support or real love. There is never any psychological or mental settling down.

When you are young, if you jump around a little bit, that is all right. But when you get a little older, it is time to mature and know that life and relationship are an art.

Both people in a relationship are players of themselves, a musical instrument. There is also an invisible instrument that is the relationship, and both of you are players of that instrument. It is important to pay attention and care for that relationship.

If you have a series of relationships with different people, the physical excitement of sex is short, but the liability or side effect is heavy and strong. The liability or side effect is the undermining of your health and the strength of life in different aspects. Once you see there is no long benefit from that type of hitchhiking life, see what areas of your personality you can improve so that you can enjoy a longer lasting friendship or relationship.

Your constant considerateness, sensitivity, and sincerity in a relationship bring forth good music. Your self-control, self-discipline, tolerance, acceptance, and assistance are all important.

I would like to give an example of where self-control is important. A piano or other instrument only has seven notes: Do, Re, Mi, Fa, So, La and Ti. In playing a human relationship, there is a large number of subtle, unheard notes. If you touch the wrong key, you hear an awful sound. I mean, if you talk about an area of the other person's thinking or experience that has some degree of sensitivity, the response may be difficult. You learn to respect other people's emotions. You know what keys are untouchable, and you know what keys give you sweet sounds. How nice it is to touch them. With the untouchable keys, if you care about the other person's growth, you take the trouble, over time, to give the other person support in examining the difficult issue involved and in practicing self-healing.

When you live singly, be happy with your single life. If you are interested in living in a relationship, you have to respect the relationship and the person you are with. If you do not respect the relationship and do not think it is necessary, you will lose it. If you do not respect the person, thinking "Men are inferior and they are beneath me," or "Women are inferior and they are beneath me," you will treat them roughly like you would treat a machine. The person may not stay. Emotionally you will pass up the good life that is right in front of you and still be looking for a good life. So do not miss your good opportunity. I use the harp as an illustration for my young students, male or female. The other person is not a machine, but is more delicate than a harp.

Here is something for you to think over when you are in your quiet time. If having a relationship is not worth the trouble, then do not have one. If you would really like to have a relationship, enter into it wholeheartedly.

Chapter 3

Changing Oneself Is the Power of Solving Problems

Service Given to a Spiritual Leader who seems to suffer from sexual complication with students and clients

Master Ni: Let us see how we can inspire each other. You may ask some questions and we will discuss them.

Visitor: I would like to know whether I am being determined or stubborn. At times, I see that I want to get to a certain point and I do not know whether I am being too hard, just determined enough or too easy. It does not flow naturally for me, because I am suspicious of my determination. I think that often I am stubborn and misguided. And I need to be done with worrying about that. I need to be clear about that.

Master Ni: In personal life, if you use your determination in an effective way, it is great. A way to simplify the procedure of decision-making is to give an explanation to yourself and put an end to the long process of consideration. For example, if you explain to yourself all your different possible motives in a situation, that will help you put an end to the long process of consideration, because then you will be clear about the goal. If your vision in seeing a thing is sharp enough, determination can be expressed. It is simple and effective. If your vision is not sharp enough, if you are motivated by your own impulses without looking at the external situation clearly, your determination will lack balanced consideration. It will bring you trouble and failure in life.

Especially when you are a teacher, if anything you do connects with people or another person, you first have to guide yourself to see the whole picture. One who sees the complete picture will produce a good decision and by so doing will be successful, earning the agreement of the people around in the environment. That is called earning the agreement of the environment. Once you secure agreement, you have support.

In a joint action, if your mind is fast and if you see the picture or solution much faster than your partner, and you alone decide and act, your partner will feel that everything is being decided by you yourself. It does not matter if your decision is right; your partner will not understand. Your partner will ask you to take responsibility for it.

It does not matter if it is your wife, friend or student. Usually you need to guide the person to see the picture. When the other person sees the picture, then he or she usually finds that the only reasonable way is the exact direction that you have already arrived at in your mind. So then, when your decision is made, your determination is easily accepted. If you make other people feel you are stubborn, assertive or tyrannical, it is usually because you have taken a step too quickly.

There are two processes of decision-making in the world. One process is the military type, where a person needs to make an immediate decision without time for discussion or negotiation, there is only enough time to make a decision about what to do. The other process is the democratic type. It is ineffective, but it is often necessary that a decision is produced through tedious discussion. Maybe it is not a wise or practical way to decide things, but it is a human process.

We play the game of living in the general world. We cannot speed things up. We, who are leaders, are already far in front and can see things that the people far behind cannot see. When we make a decision to turn, they cannot see it; that causes an unhappy feeling.

There are two possible solutions. One, when you see the picture, you can tell the other person what the picture is. Let the person come to the point of seeing what is correct to do, then use an open attitude to make a suggestion. People will usually agree and they will have no feelings about your stubbornness any more. The result is the same; the process is different. The final result will be reached in a good way. If, for example, you produce the idea for a good solution, the other person is benefitted. If the other person produces a good conclusion or a good decision, you are benefitted. Usually it does not matter who makes the decision. We all can make suggestions.

The second possible solution, useful if you are a spiritual leader or teacher, is a process that gives time for students to grow, thus their minds and vision have a chance to expand. Also, they have the whole picture, so there is no feeling about your making all the decisions and leaving them out.

Q: So I put in too much energy, don't I? I put too much energy into everything.

Master Ni: In the future, just describe, talk about or discuss a matter; lead people to see the picture. Do not at first tell them what you are going to do. If you put in too much energy, it means you are unwilling to conduct yourself with self-control in the management of personal life energy. When I was younger, I felt that sometimes I had a similar problem. It was easy for me to make decisions, because I see things much faster than other people. But that is not the way to teach. Teaching is the process of leading other people to see something.

Q: Sometimes I describe things to my students so often and so many times to make sure they see it; they say it is enough, but I know they do not really see it yet. I see it, and it is as though I need them to see it as clearly as I do. It is felt to be too much.

Master Ni: If it is the case that you put out too much, just ask the question, do not give the answer; let them find the solution. Then discuss only the appropriate evaluations or judgements. That is all there is to do, and this way also saves time. If you show them the question or the problem, they can usually see the whole picture and you save yourself the trouble of making long explanations. Let them find the solution, then a decision naturally arises out of the solution.

Q: Let them see whether it works or doesn't work.

Master Ni: If you have a dispute with somebody and that person is willing to sit down to discuss it with you, surely you cannot let the other person fall. The other person would like to argue and be the winner. But you cannot let yourself fall, so you must find a way to make both sides benefit, for both sides to be the winner. Usually there is a solution that is acceptable to both sides.

Q: I take responsibility for everything.

Master Ni: To be a teacher, a the head of a family and even a responsible person, you must always take responsibility for all things to go in the right way. However, even if you let the other people help to think about a good solution for certain matters and certain questions, you are still the manager. You still need to carry it out; not only manage it, but also receive their understanding for support. Once you receive their support, how to carry out the details still depends on you.

Q: I need to find a much gentler way of being responsible.

Master Ni: Yes, that way you will attract more friends, more helpers.

There are different types of people; some are more productive and have more organized minds. You, by yourself, can have your sharpness and shrewdness when working or accomplishing something, but when you talk to a friend, you make one mistake. You see, when you are in your office, you advise your clients. Your clients totally rely on you and they do whatever you tell them to do. Now, for long years you have built certain habits that show your affection through certain types of movement. By doing so, a client may have already changed from the stage of being a client to the stage of being a friend, but you still use the same way of treating them as a client. The person cannot accept it. He thinks, "Why do you not discuss this with me and treat me as a friend, an equal?" You have not attended to the shift, that the person is now more than just a client; he is your friend.

If there comes a time when you cannot see that person any more, you must still treat him as a friend. You must have the attitude, "Okay friend, it is time for you to move ahead. Whether it is right or wrong, we can talk about anything; it is time." You are not doing any more service for him. Maybe he can do a service for you.

If, for example, one of your students thinks you are too strong, this means he has gone from the client or student stage to the friend stage. Before, he needed your strength; afterwards when he does not feel he need it, your extra kindness, care and love is a burden to him and is not needed.

Other people who are also teachers may experience friction with you, because each one's personal view of doing business is different. You like to have total control; others also like to have the total control.

There are two ways to support the work that needs to be done and to get along with each other. One way is for you to put part of the responsibility under the other person's control. If he does it, you do not need to spend energy on that. Or you manage the whole thing your way. Otherwise, you can use his way. You let him help, and if his way is not doing very well, then you suggest your way. People will open up to you if you are open to them in this manner.

Q: So that could be why things have not been going so smoothly?

Master Ni: A certain person did not open up to you; instead, he closed tightly. He only felt that you were too strong, I believe. If you make others feel that you are too strong, then they will also like to be strong and controlling, and begin to act that way. Then you will perceive that they are too strong. Right?

It is not a one-sided problem. To correct matters between the two of you, say to yourself, "I am more achieved, so I would like to increase my capacity for more tolerance." First spell out the situation; then, even if you know how to solve the problem, let him suggest his way to do it. Listen to what he says. If he answers and his suggestion or idea is really close to your idea, then do not argue, just do it that way, and all will be nice. If he says his way and it is not right, then you show your picture. Tell him the way to do it and check out whether it is okay with him. If he comes up with a better solution, then by all means go along with it.

When you do that, people will say, "The decision was made by us together." It is not that you alone made the decision. Do you understand? That is the democratic type of leadership.

Generally speaking, the most effective type of leadership is a wise monarchy. There are good monarchies and bad monarchies. A good monarchy that makes beautiful, excellent decisions, is effective and saves lots of time and problems. The problem with monarchy is that there were few times in history when there were good, wise monarchies. I do not totally reject it; monarchy is a good system, but it all depends on who is the monarch.

I think this is no problem. If you would like to manage a small group and unify your personal management, it will be easier for you. It is good that the other teacher has his own center and you have your own. That is totally agreeable.

I do not listen to anybody who talks about you. Even if they attack your stubbornness or assertiveness, I do not mind, I accept that. Sometimes if people are too shrewd or too quick, then they will make people think differently about them. If the people who disagree with you wish to do so, they can themselves establish their own centers for teaching. If they do not, then forget it.

The only thing I do not value is a person who only can comment on others but cannot do anything himself; that is negative. If a person comments that you do not do well, and says, I would do it better than you, then all right, let him show you, let him do it. This is the world's work, it is not only individual work.

It would decrease the friction just to slow down and let people see things on their own. Talk first. If there is any small trouble with your family or any person, talk with them first. And also, never hold an attitude like, "I am going to bend you to my view." Never think that.

I believe when you show your picture to a student or somebody else, they feel that you are bending them. You do not let them do it or see it. You bend them. They feel that because you still express yourself too strongly. You put out too much. You express to them, "I won't do this, you can't do that." That shows you do what you want and cut off their joining energy. Instead, it is better to discuss things point by point with people. Then usually it is agreeable to them.

For an individual who grows up in a free society, it is important to be determined and definitive to protect the fact of your individuality. If you are determined, you will not let other people manage you. But when you become a leader, you totally need to change. On the one hand you need to be determined. But on the other hand, you need to listen to people. Let all people talk and have a chance to express themselves and exercise their intelligence first. Then, you can be the last one to have the say.

You need to make yourself say, "I am just nuts, everyone else is a sage." But you are not nuts. Naturally accept that without putting anything over them. It is the easy way to do it. This is Taoist philosophy; you can read more in Lao Tzu about how to be a leader.

Q: When I look to see why I am so strong with people, I find it is an internal strength. It does not come across in the words, but the people feel it. And I think it is because if they make any mistake, it becomes my fault. I am at fault.

Master Ni: Yes, you are overprotective. When children are in their teens, they say, "I already know what you are going to tell me." To avoid conflict, parents do not say too much to them. We just give them the general direction and let them do things their way to reach it. Now, if you have a chance, when they are looking for advice, you can talk to them. They are too young and too proud until they are in the years of maturity. It does not matter whether it is your daughter or your son; unless they ask, it is better not to give advice. Even if they ask, do not give too much. If you give too much, they immediately feel you are trying to manage them.

Q: I think I try to exercise control in order to make sure that people do not make mistakes because when my younger sister was little, my mother always told me to be responsible for her and to be protective. I learned to do that, because if I did not, my mother would become angry with me. I still have that training but I need to let go of it and trust that people will do what they must. If they don't, it is all right. They will change it.

Master Ni: It comes to the verge on psychological patterning, first by your mom, then you transfer the habit to your contacts. You need to change; you need to detach from it. Like the independent attitude of teaching Tao, always offer the best teaching. Remind your students to listen to what you say or carefully read about it from a book and tell them to use it; that is useful. If, at the moment, people are not wise enough or not clear enough to understand what you have read from books or directly from what you say, accept that. Next time they will understand, but do not demand the flower too soon. Teaching cannot demand any immediate response or result. Immediate response does not matter; it is a process of growth for people.

It is similar when you do business. If you invest or do business, you need to check yourself out first. "Do I have the strength to make the investment?" If you make the investment, do not expect a quick return. Be prepared to accept the external, unexpected circumstances.

Q: Also, I think that I am too ambitious, not for personal gain, but in order to justify my life. It seems I need to justify my life instead of just living my life and doing it the best way I know how. I need something to separate that out.

Master Ni: That is not natural. That comes from using external learning for too long, always needing to check out what you do or say with the external authorities or whatever conception is in your mind. The interpretation is not direct. It is the indirect way.

The direct way is just be it, do it, that is all. Then if you do it, and wonder about doing it wrong, or being wrong, it means you still are not following your spiritual nature. We say that in our spiritual nature, we are a small universe. The entire universe is a big model of our life. We ourselves are a small shape or form of life. In our head, we have a high level spirit. In the middle, we reach all human people with middle level spirits. In the lower part of the body, we have the lower spirits. There are also intellectual spirits. If the intellectual spirits are too strong, then you make people feel you are competing with them, or if the intellectual spirits are too tight, sharp or shrewd, you create a kind of contention. Sometimes the lower spirits do sex; there are also sex spirits. If the sexual spirits are too strong, then they bring harm to the upper two levels of spirits and cause them to suffer.

Now please let me touch the focus of this meeting. You seem to avoid touching your real problem. Although your questions relate to teaching and managing students and friends, practically that is not your problem. Your problem is that you do not know how to manage your strong sexual desire and energy. I have heard that you have been involved with too many women, having an amazing number of relationships at the same time. Thus, whatever advice I give to you, my response will concentrate on the matter of sex. Nothing is more important to you at this time.

The natural way is for the three spirit levels to support our lives without any single part making trouble or causing the other two parts to suffer. There is no good or bad, there is only the imbalance. The result turns out to be suffering. Your head suffers and your mind suffers. That often happens to young people or people who are too strong sexually.

Please keep in mind that the type of spirits that are active can sometimes differ with climate. In the northern hemisphere, the practices done will be different from those done in the south. Northern people live more in dry air and the spiritual arrangement is usually astringent. Southern people live in wet air. They are more fleshy, so they will naturally have a sexual tendency.

In ancient times, some northern people worshipped Heaven, the head in our body. But in southern countries, they worship the reproductive organs. You cannot say it is wrong. Both practices have nothing wrong with them; they are the natural effects of the energy responses in the south and the north. But our spirit can grow the wisdom to know in all circumstances what is the better way to manage or do something without harming the entire life being. What you do is not a matter of right and wrong, moral and immoral; it is only that personally and spiritually each person needs to look for harmony and balance among all aspects of his being.

Because modern people mostly have strong intellectual spirits as well as strong sexual spirits, my teaching focuses on helping people's high spirits find the right way through intellectual understanding. The teaching of Tao includes all aspects of life and spirituality, so perhaps I should also teach about the lower sphere of spirits: sex. However, if I do so, I will be extending beyond the focus of my work. I have set my focus in the single direction of spiritual development to cover all instead of in multiple directions.

Indian people are spiritual people. They have different forms of worship and what they worship affects their lives differently. For example, the southern Indian people worship Shiva, the low sphere of spirits. It is a strong deity, a spiritual image for the entire region. Those people carve stone or gather soil or sand and shape it in the form of an erect penis. Everywhere they do penis worship.

My tradition teaches the transformation of our sexual energy. We practice sublimation instead of totally putting our energy into this kind of pursuit. I do not make Taoist tantra or dual cultivation as the main practice in order to allow for achievement at different stages. We cannot sit here judging what is wrong and what is right. I do not think it is correct to condemn it. The correct way to describe these practices is to say they are a natural spiritual expression. The secret of the immortals, however, is to not do it. They still have the internal energy intercourse, which produces high pleasure, more than external sex. By not doing sex too much, you still maintain your strong energy without causing impotence. Abstinence from sex enables them to live transcendentally, not just think transcendentally. If you wish to attain the free soul and the flying soul, you must take a different direction from sexual enjoyment.

Choosing a type of practice depends on your own growth and wisdom; how much you have achieved or what depth you have reached. Do not be managed by the spirits, but rather be managed by your own growing wisdom. You see, that is the important thing. Other people's judgements, objections or attacks should not change you; only change yourself by means of your own wisdom.

I have not only learned the spiritual practice of one level, I also learned the practices of the other two higher levels. When I organize my own practice, I find the balanced way without causing harm to the upper two levels' deities, spirits or high gods.

Q: Could you please clarify this?

Master Ni: There are gods everywhere in the universe, but gods have different manifestations. There is nothing wrong with worshipping the reproductive organs; without them there would be no human people or life in the world. It is precious, it is spiritual, it is sacred, it is holy. When a man becomes old, to have no erection means vitality is gone and approach to death. Surely the erection is worshipped. Why not worship it? Both the head as the mind and the body as the impetus are part of human life; each are valuable. We should not harbor unnatural views about it, but how we apply them to our own life is a function of our own wisdom.

The Indian people who worship in this way ask anything from Shiva: money, love, power, etc.. They make offerings and are sincere. Shiva is a spirit at a different level from the other two higher levels, comprising the intellectual spirits and the spiritual spirits. But we have to find internal harmony. Harmony is Tao. Thus, do not let one part of your being cause trouble for other parts of your being. Do not let one group of spirits cause trouble for other spirits.

The well-being of an individual life and the well-being of the world are under the same law. It is not wise to let one sector of demand cause harm to the entire life.

Whatever you practice always affects your life. The different natures of the practices will affect you differently. One of my spiritual friends, before he became achieved at the beginning of his fifties, was involved with sexual practices and worship. It is a part of life and he was sexually very strong, which naturally made him look for sexual ecstacy. Because he was one never to stay in one place, he continued to study the other levels of spiritual development. Before, he could not really understand it, but slowly his level rose and he could understand the higher spiritual teaching. So then he understood. He decided he was not going to do the same old sexual habit any more.

What happened? He was a spiritual person. So when he engaged in sex, many sexual spirits came to join the sexual action and activity. In the universe, there is that level of gods who come together for sex at the same time; flesh and spirits enjoy the same thing, you see. When he stopped, he thought to himself, "I am not going to do that any more." Even without praying in a human voice, the spiritual world already heard it, so the sexual gods all came together to make a strong objection - a spiritual person's voice is so strong, it is like thunder - "We made all the arrangements; there will be a thousand girls coming to you, why should you stop?" The spirits do it with the spirits through the human body because they do not have physical bodies. But you are the one who takes responsibility. The woman does it and the woman is not necessarily only herself, the woman there; it is also an occasion for the spirits.

If you understand the spiritual world deeply, you know that all life has similar interests, until the life goes up one step in its spiritual evolution. What you call liberation from the mind is not practical; liberation from physical pressure is necessary. Physical pressure is spiritual pressure. You do not do sex; the gods on the low level push you to do it.

It is your choice. You need to work to liberate yourself and undo that tight knot you made before. This is true of any behavior pattern you wish to change. Unless you escape that disaster, you will still come back to do it, if you allow yourself to do it. But it is not a suggestion from me that you should not do it. It is not. You need to make a decision.

Once you grow up a little more, you will see that the spiritual world has different levels. "Let me enjoy health, peace, the invisible but abundant fruit I can enjoy in the high spiritual level." You might try the way of sublimation too.

Q: I need to make this move, I have to make my sexual energy uplifted by the correct practice as you described.

Master Ni: Nobody can help you, only you yourself can make the change. I have heard about your having so many relationships. Yet, people can change themselves and learn about spiritual achievement. This has been done by many people and witnessed by their friends. They cultivated themselves. They attained many experiences. Those experiences I offer to other people so they will be benefitted, the same as I was benefitted by my spiritual friends and the ways in which they achieved in my tradition.

An achieved one told me it takes many years. Sometimes he liked sex, sometimes suddenly he stopped and said to himself, "I need to gather back my spiritual energy, so I will not do it." Sometimes temptation came and he did it again. So the spiritual life of an achieved one, before he is totally achieved, is up and down, up and down. Troublesome reincarnation endlessly happens to a soul, creating many lifetimes. It is similar to making this lifetime totally an experience of up and down, down and up, life and death, death and life of the sexual desire, in an endless sexual struggle. It takes a long, long time to ascend above this cycle. When humans have sex, it is not as simple as when a butterfly does it with another butterfly. Human sex almost always comes accompanied by problems. Practically, in your life, there is no time schedule as to when you decide to give up sex. You are really only finished with it when your internal voice says, "I have done enough. I have learned that if there is any benefit to this, I have already experienced it. If there is no benefit, if it is only loss, I will stop now." Your internal voice tells you when it is time to go on to something higher. You know when it is time to stop doing something because you just do not wish to do it anymore.

In the Catholic church, they have definitely decided that the priests cannot have sex. But then some priests masturbate, have homosexual activity, or take care of all the widows in their parishes. These things are often heard about, they are not imagination. That is why in this Tradition, we say that external demand does not work. Only when something comes from inside you according to how much you have grown, can change happen. That is the reality.

I can only show you a different reality; you can choose when you are ready. It is your stage. If you are ready to change, that is nice; if you are not ready, there is no demanding.

Q: I find it difficult not to see these things momentarily as defeats and I need to see it just as it is and know that now I need to change, and that I need to ride through it by guiding my sexual force for higher purposes.

Master Ni: Spiritual sexual practice is very strong. But each individual's sexual energy is spiritual energy. It can cause a response in partners, meaning, that when your sexual energy is active and your psychic energy is high, you will find women coming to you. In just one moment, things happen. Sexual impulse cannot be controlled and well transformed at that time, so it is hard at that time to make a change. It is easy for a student to join or learn a sexual practice; he can become a special practitioner. The most responsive level in the spiritual world is sexual practice. I do not teach that; I learned it and know about it. However, once you decide to cut that off, it is an achievement.

If somebody tries to change himself by using a mantra or invocation which really means: "I need to kill my lusty ghost, lusty ghost, lusty ghost," he will find that it has the opposite effect, he will always come back to do it. The lusty ghost may be stronger. If a person really wants to change, he has to use words that have a different focus, like: "I want to improve my own well being," or "I like to give my service to the world," or "Let me maintain my inner peace."

Q: So I need to make this decision.

Master Ni: It is not a decision, it is a growth. If it is a decision, it may fail. This moment, if you decide you are not going to see your girlfriend any more, maybe the next moment you will say, "Well, seeing her once in a while is okay," and so you go back again. It is not my teaching. My teaching has no insistence, because it depends on a different level. We have different levels.

Q: So it is to see the order or benefit of the growth and then to grow for that.

Master Ni: When I was young, my teacher knew I did not have time to waste and needed the final words. The teacher just said to the other adult students, "If you cannot live, if you become crazy without sex, just do it." The teachers do not like to see you become crazy or run into danger if you do not sleep with the opposite sex. They would rather see you safe and with a sexual partner. But they also say, "If you can do it, then live without sex." There is no demanding.

So it is a matter of growth. Also, if you study astrology, you will find that some people's charts show a greater strength in some parts than others. All have different tendencies. If somebody can only become a great lover among women, it is indicated by the natal chart. There is no way to decide upon only one way of teaching. We can only help students however they come, from whatever background and with their different thoughts. What is the best way for each student is not the best unified way for the teacher. It is not like religions that have a big program that includes everybody. In Taoism, there is no one unified program. We have lots of different practices, according to the stage of the student, as the best way for him or her.

Q: What would be a good practice for me now?

Master Ni: According to your physical condition, I would say, you should decrease sex, start to retreat from it. Because of your age and physical condition, it is wise to use your energy to help your own life. If you choose to live in the south where the weather is hot, it will be hard for you to give up sex. You must have sex to kill the fire in your head. In that case, perhaps you should do a Taoist sexual practice. Certain deity worship, certain rituals can be done to transform sexual activity into a spiritual ritual. You have to be watchful. Generally speaking, it is wise not to do sex with your clients or your students. Because you, as an instructor, do the other level of teaching, it will confuse them. But you might ask, "There are lots of teachers who do this, who do they do it with?" It is true, they do it with students, but it is a different practice; you have to choose a different way to do it.

Q: What practices are there to do? What I do now is spend a long time each day looking at myself, examining myself, going over myself, like a dentist with a pick, looking for the soft spots. And I look and I look. I work with the I Ching a lot. I pray every day and I work very hard to help people.

Master Ni: I understand. I personally feel that your spiritual nature is precious. You will continue to help people and at the same time to achieve yourself. My subtle teaching, my subtle guidance to you is to make you work, because you are already intellectually achieved. Through this way, maybe you will understand more and do better. I take a slow step; whatever I produce I let you work on, to make you understand better. Maybe you will see a new vision of life. That is a safer method than if I were to list ten different items of practice; you would become confused. You would not know what to choose, what is good or bad.

Q: Thank you, it is working.

Master Ni: In this short meeting, I do not think I have helped you sufficiently. Some useful information which I recommend that you read is the pamphlet called the *Heavenly Way.* The revised and enlarged version is called *The Key to Good Fortune: Refining Your Spirit.* A thorough study of this book combined with working to realize its contents will bring practical help to start your new fortune. It brings the hope of achieving oneself to be with a trouble-free spirit in this lifetime.

Chapter 4

Correct Sexual Fulfillment

1
For Men

When you are young and on the threshold of adulthood, it is easy for you to become sexually excited. I would like you to know that your sexual energy is also the energy that fuels your brain. Generally, young people are sensitive and are easily tempted by the external to seek sexual fulfillment. During this time, a young person particularly needs to be on guard against external influences or temptations. If you are male, this is an important time to concentrate on your studies or exercises to achieve your development in all important aspects of your life. At this age, if you abuse yourself or perform incorrect sexual expression, you will shorten your life. Then, like a defeated rooster, you cannot attain high intellectual development or build a strong foundation for longevity.

If you are an adult, you may wish to find a partner with whom you feel you have rapport sexually. However, if the other person does not offer a harmonious response, do not engage in sex with her. A violent or forceful way of doing sex not only damages the other person, but yourself also. It is not a way to solve your sexual energy. If you do not have a partner, your sexual energy should be conducted to a creative area such as building a good life for yourself. If you do that, you will naturally be more attractive to women than if you make sexual enjoyment your life goal.

It is important to understand yourself. Some people are not suitable for marriage or full expression in a sexual relationship. They need to look for their correct life expression, then concentrate on that direction that would best help them. Men really must learn to develop sexual control. It is not correct for women to perform sex at certain times of the feminine cycle nor to prolong sexual fun after the age of 40 if they wish to have better health in old age. Also, a man cannot have sex with a woman at the time of her ovulation if he does not choose to have children.

Q: Can we consider birth control as an alternative, good or bad?

Master Ni: Birth control is intelligent achievement of human people. It is correct for people to consider whether bringing a new life in the world will bring happiness or suffering to themselves and to the new life. Therefore, there is involvement of possible serious responsibility. Some spiritual teachings consider sex to be bad. If this were true, then celibacy would be the only way and birth control would not be considered as good by them. Using birth control implies approval of sex. However, whether it is appropriate for birth control to be used or not is totally dependent upon the situation. There are many kinds of birth control ranging from natural methods to chemical or artificial birth control. Some of my other books discuss some Taoist methods of birth control along with correct sexual instruction.

Whether sex is done with the purpose of having children or not, a man must be delicate in how he performs the act. If a woman is not ready, a man's mechanical penetration can damage her organ. A woman who already has a physical illness or other weakness, should definitely avoid sex. If she persists, she will only deplete her personal life energy.

Good sexual fulfillment is not found with a prostitute. In that sort of business transaction, the main element is missing: rapport. Good sexual fulfillment needs rapport to encompass to the four points of the physical, mental, emotional and spiritual to achieve complete harmony. Even if a couple is not deeply involved, general rapport is still very important.

For a man to engage in rape is not only socially unacceptable, but also shortens his personal life and damages his personal spiritual reality. By your own knowledge, you should not do it. It is very unwise.

In life, making money and making love are very similar. Both require the right approach. The wrong approach is not beneficial.

2
For Women

I recognize that women are physically and emotionally a little more complicated than men. First I would suggest that if you wish to establish a long term relationship with someone, you first need to look for somebody you respect. If you respect your partner, even if the material support is not too good, you will still have a happy life together. If you do not respect the other person as your mate, then perhaps you do not respect yourself either. A person without self respect does not put limits on her behavior by being selective in a relationship. Once you lose self respect, it is dangerous, because you do not treat yourself well, but always cause trouble.

Not only is sexual hygiene and safety about disease important, but also who you are with. If you make money from prostitution for your survival, I suggest you look for another approach to survival. This is not making good money. If a person overdoes sex, it is easy to observe that their system becomes loose, not tight any more. Dark circles appear under the eyes, the face becomes puffy, and the vision is not sharp any more. The forehead may be dark or there may be some pimples on the face or lips. These all indicate that you have damaged yourself sexually because you did not respect yourself. If you still love your life, you immediately need to stop all the old habits and cleanse yourself.

There is nothing more important than personal dignity. Having dignity is equal to owning a kingdom. If you do not have dignity, even if you own a kingdom, you are marked as someone of low personality and your life opportunity is wasted by not valuing your spirit.

There are lots of spiritual things you need to learn besides not overextending your physical self through sex. Sex is a short-lived part of life energy, although it is essential. If you learn how to cultivate yourself, and maintain yourself decently and suitably, I think you are almost equal to any sage in any time.

3
For Men and Women

With the purpose of advising you not to damage your sexual energy, I would like to talk some more about sexual energy. People go through different stages of life: infancy, childhood, youth, early adulthood, middle age, later adulthood and old age. Sometimes a human life can be divided into segments of years to define each stage. However, each individual has a different internal time system, so sometimes counting years is not definitively accurate.

Both by external observation and internal understanding, sexual energy has different stages of growth and has different functions depending on the time of life. The condition of their sexual energy determines people's health in different stages. So sexual energy basically is the foundation of an individual's life.

The ancient Taoists developed knowledge and techniques of longevity and spiritual immortality. Both longevity and immortality depend upon sexual energy.

When people are young, before the growth of their sexual energy, gender attributes are not seen. Even though the baby and young child have sexual organs, the nature of the young person is neutral. Once the sexual energy grows inside of the body, however, the feature of the gender can distinctly be seen. Normally, this occurs at about age 16 for a boy and 14 for a girl, except in warmer climates, where the maturity of internal sexual aspects occurs much earlier.

However, fruit that ripens early also falls sooner from the tree. It is unnatural to hurry one's sexual maturity. Any external interference causes trouble. Hurrying up the growth of the young life will also hurry the passing away of the life.

My teaching focuses and concentrates on the value of life. The knowledge can help you to grow healthily, and to live longer and enjoy more. Also, you can possibly bring more positive contributions into your life and other people's lives.

Sometimes, when young people start to feel sexual energy growing inside them, they hurry for sexual satisfaction such as masturbation or real sexual contact. That is almost like cutting or damaging the root of a young tree. It does not matter, man or woman, when you are young, if you enter adult life too fast or too early, it hurts your root. If you conserve that energy, it can become the foundation of longevity and provide good health in old age. The spiritually ambitious can also become spiritually immortal because its foundation is also sexual energy.

4
The Value of Sexual Energy for Health

I would like to give you a little understanding about spiritual immortality. Once you understand, and you know there is such a thing as immortality, maybe your evaluation of life will be different.

Let me first talk about the importance of sexual energy. Sexual energy provides a protective shield around a person known as the immune system. A person's immune system provides natural resistance to the changes of climate. During seasonal changes, sometimes the natural environment creates tiny entities in the air called viruses. They are invisible. There are many types of viruses. We are born as a natural life. If we maintain ourselves well, we are endowed by nature with due power of resistance to sickness caused by invasion of virus, bacteria or whatever. This protective energy is called wei chi, protective energy. Everybody has it; it comes from your sexual energy. If people lose it, they die. So, if the immune system of a young life has a problem, the baby dies. During the growth of a child, that energy not only keeps the child well, but it also provides for bodily growth.

Mental maturity is slow. It takes many years, perhaps 40, 50 or 60 years, for the mind to become ripe to receive naturally balanced vision. Most people die before their mind reaches its full maturity. One's sexual energy also is the energy that powers the mind.

Sexual energy has a season, like trees, in which to grow fruit. When a child is a teenager, there is no mistaking the growth of the sexual energy, because it begins to disturb the youth.

That energy that disturbs your sexual organ is the same imperceptible energy that surrounds the whole body just outside and inside of the skin, the wei chi. It is like the first line of soldiers which fights any possible invasion by virus or bacteria. However, this energy can be depleted through masturbation or sex. This is not talking about abnormal sex, but normal sex too. After you have sex, if you pay attention, you will feel that your energy is low and you can easily become sick or catch a cold. This happens because the upper part, the protective chi, becomes depleted. It is as if you are deflated, because your energy goes down and out. After sex, many men or women catch a cold. If you have a cold, it means you need to rebuild your protective chi. If you are already sick, and you immediately have sex again, you will only cause a disturbance or disorder of your immune system. What will happen? Because there is no protective energy around your lungs, in your breathing system, you could get pneumonia if it becomes serious.

Some time ago, tuberculosis was serious trouble for people. Some tuberculosis patients have told me that their sexual energy was so strong that they could not stand it. In normal people, sexual energy is still controllable. People who have tuberculosis do not look strong, but the congestion is stronger than usual in their sexual organs because the energy gathers there. The nature of the disease pulls all the energy from the rest of the body to the sexual organs. Usually people who catch tuberculosis have weakened their lungs and immune system by masturbation or overdoing sex, so the disease was easily caught.

I hope this helps you understand that sexual activity is like picking fruit. It has its proper time. It cannot be done constantly. Yes, when young, one can have it with a more frequent rhythm. But at an older age, picking the fruit needs to slow down. You cannot pick the fruit too often. The foundation of Taoist learning is to slow down your activity. When you are older, then stop it altogether. You should not use any external thing to prolong your pleasure. It is valuable to know this.

5
Spiritual Value of Sexual Energy

More valuable is to know that, not only can your sexual energy become protective chi, it can also transform inside you to become a subtle entity called a spirit. It is totally provable by my practice. This is scientific, but it cannot be made public. I talk about it, but how can I teach it? I will eventually find a way, maybe through a seminar or some other means. If you keep the sexual energy inside the body, naturally or through a special cultivation, it will gather together to form a tiny spiritual entity, which is one step higher than general chi.

Protective chi can be proven by the push hands exercise of T'ai Chi. In doing this, the chi can be expressed as higher power than physical strength. The idea that the soft can overcome the strong is proven. Surely, this is not a direction of high spiritual development, but the foundation is the same: it comes from chi. This strength can come from general physical energy after it is transformed to be something higher: chi.

So sexual performance, physical energy and the better mind of high productivity creation all have their common basic energy as chi. When you maintain energy or chi within the body, it assists you to have higher performance in all aspects of life function. In general, it transforms to become a warmth that spreads throughout the entire body. Then it moves around the skin, inside the muscles, between the muscles and the skin and on the membrane surrounding the organs. That is how the chi goes everywhere within.

The first step is to take care of sexual energy by being frugal. Sexual energy is important for general health. The first step or stage is to know the importance of having a cyclic or rhythmic performance of sex rather than having no order and doing it too much, too frequently.

In the second step, this energy can assist your physical work and help your health. It can transfer to produce children or other types of productivity. Thus, instead of using sexual energy in sex, you use it as general physical strength and the energy to support health.

The second step is to change sexual energy into mental energy. Once this energy becomes higher, the benefit is much greater. It will render a greater service. So the second step is to move the chi from the low sphere to the middle sphere. Your sexual energy and your general physical chi transfers to become a strong mind. With a strong mind, you do not easily get irritated or become emotional. Emotion is another type of mentality. Instead, the creative mind becomes smart or sharp, and all this presents a good mentality. The real foundation of the mind is still from sexual energy.

Once you further transform the sexual energy to mentality by studying and using the mind, that will be more powerful than what physical energy can produce. All civilizations and positive cultural creations are produced by mind. Good politics, good social systems and good economic systems are all produced by a beautiful mind. But there is no beautiful mind unless a person knows how to conduct sexual energy to be good, creative mentality.

The third step is approaching spiritual immortality. Spiritual immortality is possible because this chi or energy, whether applied in sex, physical work or mental work, all has the same one source. When that energy is channelled internally, using a special practice or done naturally, a spiritual entity can be formed within the body. Immortality is going one step further after you gather all that foundation and have created the spiritual entity. Then all spiritual energy becomes one complete spiritual being like yourself. That spiritual being does not have a physical body, but a spiritual body. It was produced by your sexual energy that was transformed to be something else. That energy, before it became sexual liquid, before it became muscular strength used in labor work, before it was expressed in your mind as a poem, did not have a form. It was pure energy. From that foundation of spiritual cultivation, you naturally produce numerous spiritual entities within. I mean that you produce more than one spiritual entity that forms the complete spiritual body.

Typically, when people die, their soul leaves the body and the rest of their energy scatters. It scatters in nature, in the trees or the air, or sinks into the ground if it is too heavy. Because the physical body is gone, it has nowhere to stay. So the possibility of immortality arises when a person, through a certain practice, gathers the energy inside to firstly form the spiritual entity. Then, one step further is to gather the small spiritual entity to become a large spiritual being. It can be your size, or unlimited, depending upon one's personal cultivation. The spiritual body is not measured by size, it is measured by the sharpness or effectiveness of its power.

Mostly this discussion is intended to get you to have some understanding of the importance of sexual energy. Immortal practice happens step by step. You get a little bit of achievement, you learn a little bit, you prove a little bit, you believe a little bit, then you go further a little bit. Then step by step, you become more and more achieved. That is called actualization of spiritual life. It is a different process than figuring out a mathematical formula that you write on paper and then are finished with.

The main point here is the important information about correct sexual fulfillment. Do not destroy your energy foundation by too much or improper sex. If once you destroy your foundation, there is nothing more for you to achieve in other aspects. This is truthful knowledge; one's life foundation starts from that part of energy.

You know, I almost put all the value on spiritual immortality. That will mislead you. I need to carefully tell you something more. Each individual was a small spirit, produced from nature, part of the spirit produced by the father and mother's sexual energy. With the combination of both yang energy from the sun and yin energy from the father and mother's sexual energy, comes the possibility of a complete spiritual entity, the spiritual function inside of each individual. It is precious and respectable to be a human life. This valuable human life is the real god, but not a powerful monster type of God. You need to respect it. Do not turn away from the real god to lower yourself down to the false conceptual creation of external religious teaching. What the conceptions do, at their best, is to hint that you are the god or goddess. You are precious, you contain all the energy. The entire universe lives in you, lives with you. It is a religious conception that you only need to be immortal only when you die. The true immortality is your spirit. Once you produce your spirit, and you know how to handle your spirit and your energy, you will live forever.

The universe is so big, there is always a place for our eternal survival. We talk about eternal survival, but we cannot neglect our survival now. You need to respect your life, and do not do anything extra to disturb your good condition of completeness as a universal natural being.

As human life, we are on the top of the animal world. Human energy is more complete than that of any animal life. Human life has more potential for development than any animal life. This is the reality. There is spiritual energy in animals too, but any animal that wishes to be spiritually evolved and go to a higher stage has as its goal to become a human being. After they become human, then they can go higher and take the next step. We are already in this stage and have received the spiritual benefit of a better position for further spiritual evolution.

Dear friends, your life is most precious, your life is most respectful. Life is made by energy. Your energy in concrete shape is sexual energy. A person may have a head but no spiritual energy. That energy all starts from the lower, sexual organs, and moves up. So I am telling you when you value your life, when you take care of your life, you should also be careful not to abuse your sexual energy. Once your sexual energy is destroyed, all high potential will be badly affected. This is my earnest learning.

6
Management of Sexual Energy

Q: Master Ni, how can a man control his sexual desire? Would you kindly give us some practical suggestions? (This question is from a male student).

Master Ni: I was told that today's situation of sex between man and woman has unhealthy aspects. Many women are raped. Thus, I would like to give some instructions and suggestions to those who are interested in spiritual improvement from the viewpoint of spiritual awareness.

First, if a man does not wish to be sexually tempted, he needs to watch his diet. For those who have strong sexual desire, a very light diet may greatly help their self-control. The healthiest change for young desirous people, as well as for people of all ages, is to become a strict vegetarian. When a man's bodily desire is too strong, he may lose his balance and slip into criminal tendencies.

For all men wishing to calm their sexual fire, I suggest eating meals consisting of one or two pieces of bread with peanut butter and a similarly proportioned amount of steamed vegetables. Three meals of this each day can keep you strong and healthy, while not causing a big financial burden nor requiring too much time for cooking. However, do not overeat peanut butter, because it will cause hormonal stimulation and make you desirous as well as give you pimples. Sensitive people should use cashew butter instead of peanut butter. Overeating peanut butter will also make you sluggish or heavy in weight. Any nut butter has the same effect if overeaten, but some are milder than others.

Do not change to this diet suddenly, but do it gradually. After you eat such a diet for a while, you will see how much better you feel. If once you form a good habit in any area, but especially in eating, it will pay or reward you by how you live. You can find whole grain bread almost anywhere, along with peanut butter, good water, and green vegetables in season. Steam the vegetables but do not oversteam them. If they turn out yellowish, they are oversteamed. Eat the bread with the peanut butter and vegetables and drink the water, and that will make your good energy strong. Try to manage how much and what comes into your belly with flexible adjustment as part of self-control.

An even more effective way to curb sexual desire through diet is to partially fast. This can put you above your sexual demand. At least, never eat until you are too full. That is overeating. It causes the blood to stay in the lower part of the body, and the sexual organs become congested with energy.

Any good physical measure should be adopted, based on the spiritual learning and practice I have described in my other work. A good and suitable diet, but not rigid practice, will make your desire much more controllable without affecting your physical strength. The adjustments in your diet depend upon the knowledge you attain.

If you are subject to many kinds of situations for eating, at least try to avoid shrimp, oysters, garlic and other stimulating foods, because they excite sexual energy, and make it difficult for you to handle yourself.

Those foods are good for older Taoists or older people who wish to restore their physical health for the purpose of spiritual cultivation. They can eat the opposite of young people. In other words, older people, say those over 60 with good self-control, can eat some meat, shrimp, oysters and garlic in combination with the bread, peanut butter and steamed vegetables. However, do not overdo eating meat or shellfish, because they can cause high cholesterol levels. These foods are still not enough to help the sexual energy be expressed in normal life expression. These foods do not provide enough sexual energy to maintain the life of an older person. Spiritual cultivation is still necessary to maintain the normalcy of life.

If you are young and you use your energy in the direction of sexual madness, then eating foods such as shrimp and garlic is not productive or helpful to your life. Sex is like a bottomless pit; it can never be filled up. At the right age, you can rhythmically and harmoniously fulfill your sexual desire, but never overdo it. If you overdo sex in your youth, when you are older, your sexual energy will become exhausted from that performance.

The value in physical life is spirit. It is produced by sexual energy sublimation. Therefore, when you maintain your body and your physical energy, you maintain your spirit. The purpose of all the physical and spiritual practices I give you in my books is to nurture your spiritual energy. I have already given a simple thing by talking about diet.

Second, pay attention to temperature. Do not dress too tightly or too warmly by using tight underwear or pants made of thick, heavy or stimulating material. The lower part of the body will become congested with blood and energy and will cause you to feel extremely desirous. Any time you cover yourself too much, such as when sleeping, you become too warm and the body heat stirs your organ. When you have great impulse, a cold water wash or bath will help your self-control.

Third, do not use alcohol or beer. It will disturb your circulation and make some parts of your body easily congested with blood. Young people already have the problem of congesting sexual energy congestion, so avoid that and any other drugs. All types of stimulants, drugs or medications should be avoided, even including herbal medicines whose properties are unknown to you. If you do not have full knowledge of its usage, and it is not prescribed for you, do not use it. Herbal medicines are for helping your physical health, and supporting your spiritual health for spiritual purpose. They are not for increasing sexual performance. Over-extending oneself in sex is the direction of most people, but is not what I recommend.

Fourth, be a self-controlled person. Do not let society conduct your life. Watching TV and movies, and reading certain books or magazines will conduct or lead you into behaviors which are not socially acceptable. Do not watch them unless you are already achieved. Once you are achieved, you do not bother to look at those distractions any more, or at least, your taste changes. When you are young, you do not know what is good to eat, good to watch or good to listen to. You just do it, and become stimulated. Then you are not the boss of yourself; you are conducted or led by something else. You are a puppet, robot or machine manipulated by someone else. Such irresponsible behavior damages your soul.

When you live in commercial society, everyone tries to influence you to do what they desire. If you do not learn to control and conduct yourself, then you give yourself up. You become a slave of the society. My suggestion is spiritual self-cultivation. Do not be conducted by this unhealthy trend of society. Do not be mislead by a commercial culture that will form your habit to buy this and that, to have more wants, or to chase after the newest fashion. I am not a person who is anti-materialistic. I do not suggest we get rid of what we have or not buy useful things that are needed. But make your decisions by yourself. Make a good choice, not for luxury or fashion, but for practical service. Buy something that is enduring, and will work for your money. Do not make yourself a slave of material things.

The fifth suggestion is to learn some Taoist movement. Jogging is still all right if you manage well, but tennis, baseball, football and working out in the gym will all make you too rigid physically. The purpose of being physically strong, as most people enjoy it, is for sex. But I recommend that you do the Taoist movement as shown in my videotapes or taught by my sons and in the affiliated Taoist centers. Those activities are balanced and help your internal circulation and secretions. They do not work much on your muscles to develop you in a partial sense, but they can help your emotional control, energy flow, coordination, balance, concentration and spiritual centeredness.

The sixth suggestion is to do spiritual learning. I always say that spiritual life should be within worldly life, but I do not mean the vulgar world. I mean, you do not depart from the world to hide in a closet, but you still can make personal choices and accept what is good in society and the world. What is your personal choice?[1]

These suggestions are valid for women and men students who aspire to spiritual growth and wish to calm sexual or emotional desire. Even though you still need to be guided, whatever you do will help your physical, mental and spiritual health and the balance of all three. It is not hard for you to achieve good health, but once you abuse it, then all aspects of your life will be depleted or destroyed.

---

[1]Please refer to Master Ni's book, *Moonlight in the Dark Night*, and read the chapter entitled, "Clear Choices: Selective or Minimum Involvement" and other discussions of spiritual learning for guidance on how to live close to the world without being entrapped by it.

7
If You Were Raped

Many years ago, I had a student who was a manager of a Japanese investment firm in Taiwan. Once he told me a true story. It was something that happened in his home town, Sen Yang, in northeast China around the 1930s. Russia had been interested in having a year-round harbor in the east beginning with the so-called Peter the Great. After the successful communist revolution in Russia, this ambition was not forgotten. Japan was also interested in northeastern China. The two countries periodically sent troops to that part of China to try to conquer it. Not only did they fight the Chinese for that territory, but often the Russians and the Japanese ended up fighting each other. Sometimes both of them were in competition, and sometimes one became superior to the other.

Once Russia sent a big army to try to gain control of the territory. One troop consisted totally of women soldiers. They were full fledged soldiers and carried rifles just like the men, and it was their task to occupy the city of Sen Yang. One day, my student and his friend were riding in the car. At the side of the road, they saw a young man laying on the ground. They went over to him to see if he was alive or not. Although the man seemed on the verge of death, he was young and it seemed that he might have a chance to recover. So they picked him up and brought him home, and helped him to regain his strength. Then they asked him what happened. He told them that a group of women soldiers had pulled him into a trench at the side of the road. There were, of course, trenches all over the city because of the war. Footsoldiers with rifles need trenches to hide in. Because that city suffered so many wars, there were many trenches by almost every road. That young man had been pulled by the woman soldiers into the trench and raped. Not just by one; it was group rape. It almost killed him.

This is something that seldom happens in China. Men raping women is also rare in China, or at least in my home town when I grew up. Now that I work in the United States, I often hear women patients or women readers of my books discussing the problem of rape. I have already done some written work to call your attention to how you can guide your own body so that you do not cause any trouble for yourself. You must guard your body like you guard your money. One woman wrote to me about such an event which had already happened. Here are two attitudes that I can recommend that may help anyone, male or female, overcome psychological damage from such a thing happening.

I believe that a person who is raped feels unhappy because it was an attack, a humiliation. It was not done by invitation, but without permission or the willingness of the other. I think this is psychological damage.

There are two attitudes about that. One woman reader who had studied Buddhism believed that the happening was the result of her karma from a past life. Perhaps she needed to pay something back to someone for what she had done previously in a past life. This is a typically Buddhist thought.

Let us examine several points of view about this subject. Firstly, human life is a transformation of a soul. Sometimes a person is shaped with flesh, sometimes a person is defleshed to become a soul again. If a soul incarnates as a man, and does not achieve excellently in obtaining social status and a woman's love or interest, sometimes its mind becomes peculiar and the person attacks a woman. If perhaps you did that in a past life, now you are the one who receives that kind of violence. This may be true. It is a wider view of life than that of the average person. That kind of understanding can be helpful. However, we could take our spiritual evolution and understanding one step higher.

Let us look at the traditional Taoist theory about this. A Taoist way to explain this kind of situation is to consider it as a natural accident. Once Chuang Tzu told a story about someone walking down the street. He said, "A person is walking down the street, and the wind blows a loose tile from the roof of a house so that it falls and hits him on the head. Who should he be angry at, the wind, the tile or the house?" What Chuang Tzu meant was that it was useless to be angry, because the tile had already fallen and nothing could be done to change that. How can this kind of attitude be applied towards a natural accident like we have mentioned? Similar to the tile falling, the occurrence was not the fault of the person to whom it happened. It was a temporary circumstance in time and space that happened due to a certain accumulation of energy unrelated to the person to whom it befell. It was a certain momentary impulse.

Some women recover quickly from such an event. They see it for what it was, take steps to protect themselves and then forget about it. But others take longer. Traditionally, we have some psychological tools or conceptions that might help those individuals. If a woman is attacked, it is helpful for her to pray for the person who did the injustice. Pray for his soul and that some day he will be enlightened and understand his error. Pray that he regrets his action and wishes you well. Have compassion for a person who does not do well in life and could be put in jail. Surely nobody welcomes such a thing happening, but a forgiving attitude will make it easier to recover. If you have that kind of spiritual quality, where you can pray for the benefit of the wrongdoer, then it also helps protect you spiritually. However, physical protection is also important and should never be neglected.

Once I witnessed some young Taoist women who lived in a high mountain. They were almost totally secluded and there were many places in which a bandit could easily hide. The women who lived there, dressed exactly like men so that people would not recognize them as women. They did not make their bodies fragrant or beautiful. Sometimes when they went out to the town or the surrounding countryside, they put dirt on their faces. They also learned martial arts. That is how they survived there.

You can find a way to protect yourself. Whatever happened, you can follow my suggestion and look for a better way to protect yourself.

An individual life being is a specific piece of life energy. Once you suffer intrusion, transgression or invasion by someone else's energy, spiritual purification is necessary to return you to a state of psychological alertness. What I call psychological alertness is restoring yourself to normal after your emotional upset. When you keep reliving the experience again and again, you keep destroying your spiritual health. That is an unwise thing to do. In the *Workbook for Spiritual Development of All People*, there is an invocation and a whole set of purifications.[2] It is helpful to read the invocations in a quiet, private place and with a quiet mind. Have a cup of pure water in front of you. When you finish one invocation, join the middle finger and thumb of the right hand at the fingertips, dip them in the water and sprinkle the water on your own head. That will change your energy.

Also, you can burn a piece of clean paper in the area around your head as a fire wash to disperse whatever bad energy has connected with you. But be careful, do not let the paper burn your hand, hair, furniture or house. If circumstances provide for it and you are in a safe place, you can build a small bonfire and walk over it. This can also help you disperse other people's energy contact with you. I mean that you can step over a low fire, but do not walk on it with your shoe. In ancient times, people did a fire ceremony in festivals. They would burn charcoal on the ground and walk on it with bare feet without burning their feet or getting blisters. The secret to being able to do this is to spread salt on the coals, but I do not suggest that you try it. The simple way is each time in your meditation, to visualize that you are burning to be nothing.

These suggestions can help you gather your energy back in one piece. After each purification, you become a better self. You can repeat any of the purifications as many times as you wish if you feel the need.

There are two different ways to handle this matter. One way to accept it as your bad karma. So now you have paid it back and it is done. Another way is to accept it as an accident that could happen to any woman. Those are means of psychological acceptance. Spiritual practice is

---

[2]See page 103, The Five Purifications; page 104 Purification of the Mouth, Purification of the Body; page 105, Purification of the Mind, Purification of the Earth; page 106, Purification of My Entire Being in Union with Heaven and Earth.)

totally different than accepting something psychologically. Spiritually, you deny it, cleanse it, wash it away and eliminate the bad energy that has attacked you.

In ancient times, a man who habitually made a woman his victim was considered to be possessed by an evil or sexually desirous ghost. It means that the person who undertook such bad behavior lost the sense of personality. If a person is a young, spiritually ignorant person, the guilt can be repented. If it becomes a habit and the person is already an adult, it is a serious spiritual defect and will cause spiritual sinking to a state of low confinement for thousands of years. My suggestion to my male readers is never to force a woman to comply with your desire. Only harmonious sex brings a certain level of energy exchange. If you force the other person to do it, there is no energy response, and no benefit at all. It will only cause your personality to fall apart and your soul to lose the potential to achieve itself.

Conclusion

For sexual fulfillment, the time must be right. The partner must be right and the way you do it must be right. I cannot rigidly decide what is right or wrong for any other person. I would rather keep open so that you can grow your own knowledge or learn from a really achieved teaching tradition. This is the knowledge to have a relationship based on happiness and the benefit of both persons.

Knowing the correct way of spiritual achievement is difficult because there are so many religions and traditions. Taoism does not seem to give one single clear instruction, because it has many sects that developed later, such as various folk Taoisms. However, the high truth is one. Although special individuals, all religions and all traditions have access to the universal high truth, they do not always catch it. Thus, incorrect teaching can be given and a student can easily be misguided.

The correct practice of sexual fulfillment or useful celibacy and the development of fanatic sexual practices are two different matters. Some practices of the sects of folk or religious Taoism directly conflict with the correct purpose of spiritual cultivation. Some sects overemphasize the importance of sex, while others promote the religious type of ascetic practice, celibacy. Neither is realistic. They are not the important practice of the Integral Way.

In learning Tao, there are many byways. The only correct way is the Integral Way or the middle way, which can guide you to a broad and everlasting direction of life, while avoiding narrow or extreme alleys.

Chapter 5

The Esoteric Taoist Practice: Natural and Spiritual Sexual Harmony

In the Tradition of Tao, we have developed many exercises, internal work and practices, herbal medicines and dietary advice to help with the restoration of sexual energy. These are mostly to help people who have a problem or have become depleted through aging. If you have normal sexual strength, that is good enough.

Unfortunately, human fantasy pushes people who already have enough sexual strength to do things to give them more. This type of over-strengthening, quickening or speeding up of sexual energy will cause a person to lose energy and age faster. For example, once I described how some Chinese men used a strip of cloth tied to their sexual organs from which they hung bricks. Each week or three days, they would increase one brick and do a swinging exercise, like the pendulum of a clock, until the male organ could carry several hundred pounds. This is really extreme and ultimately improper when you are young. Any Taoist skills for sexual rejuvenation are for people over seventy or seventy-five whose sexual energy is gone. It is to pull them back and restore function. Unfortunately, few older men are interested in restoring their sexual energy, but young people who already have more than enough energy are the ones who wish to do the practices.

One of the practices is to eat a special diet including oysters, shrimp and the sexual organs of animals. In shrimp, for example, the sexual organs and their corresponding hormones are on the head. Also, Chinese men eat the penises of snakes, lions and tigers, to the point that these animals came close to dying out.

Basically, such a special diet is for people who are in their old age and the purpose is not for sex, but to complete their depleted energy spectrum in order that they can live to a very old age. It is the sexual energy that keeps a person alive. It is a pity that few older people have knowledge of this food medicine and that many young people have this information because it has been commercialized and sold to them. This is an incorrect application of the culture of Taoism. When the learning of Tao is correctly applied, it is a wonderful thing but if incorrectly applied, it is evil. A man who can sustain himself more than several minutes in sexual activity can be considered normal. T'ai Chi Ch'uan or the Eight Treasures can increase a man's sexual energy from twenty minutes to forty minutes or more, even up to hours. That is good enough. Why does anyone still need to gather the penises of panthers, wolves or dogs? That is overdoing it; that is a remedy for older people. This is a major human undevelopment that when we are young, we like to hurry up or increase our successes.

I would like to share some of the correct information for the benefit of modern people looking for a healthy way of life. I promote sexual harmony on two levels. One level is for all people, whether they are ordinary or spiritual people. It is natural sex. Natural sex means not to use any external excitation from pictures or cultural stimulation. When you feel that your energy is full or congested, then you do it. Usually sex done in that way will bring no harm. That information is also given in my work, *Eight Thousand Years of Wisdom, Book II.* Now I have reprinted it in this book as the following, with some revision.

This talk will be in three parts. I will say something first for those of you who have sex, and then I will talk to those who are celibate and singly searching for spiritual achievement.

Let me start by saying something for the younger ones. None of you are youngsters any more, but you have been youngsters and so you will know if what you did when you were young damaged your sexual strength or not.

In the Integral Way, we view sexual energy as the root of life for human beings. From sexual energy comes the energy with which we work, read and do everything. This working energy can also be developed into spiritual energy. It is a process of step-by-step growth and transformation. If you do anything wrong with your sexual energy when you are young, then there will be a lot more difficulty than usual in your further development.

When people are young, the most important thing is not to start having sex too early. Doing that is like damaging the root of a young tree. So if you have youngsters at home, tell them not to start too early, and that good things come to people slowly.

Also, sexual life is an area in which people become too loose. In old China, there was a saying that when you are in your thirties you are a wolf and when you are in your forties you are a tiger. But many people, if their root is damaged in their youth, come to their thirties and forties and are only dead wolves and paper tigers. Today, in this modern society, both men and women have that same problem because they started their sexual life too early and did it improperly. They experienced all the excitement and enjoyment in the early part of their life and what is left after is just a worn-out body.

In any community or nation, youngsters are the foundation and future of the whole society. People should pay more attention to this fact and not tempt them through movies or television to do improper things.

The second thing that is important for youngsters to know is never to masturbate. Masturbation is worse than actual sex as far as harming the body's root because there is no feedback from the opposite sex. Because youngsters are curious and have natural bodily sensitivity, they can easily form the habit of masturbation. However, if they do so, they become nervous, isolated and slow in mind. They always take the back seat, they cannot be put in the front line of anything because they have already hurt their physical root. Boys and girls should be careful about their psychological health when they are young. All young people need to keep away from temptation, stay strong and prepare for the long span of life. Although the span of life might be relatively short, it is still valuable in all its different stages and needs to be protected.

This is all I have to say to the youngsters. My main focus is on those who are already grown. As a Taoist traditional healer, I have had many opportunities to see how people have damaged themselves when they were young, and thereby made a lot of trouble for themselves in their middle years and shortened their lives.

What is sex? Please, you tell me. Who does sex? I would say that sex is chi performance. Chi is energy. It is so subtle and so wonderful! Human life itself is chi performance. If you do not have chi, how will you live? Take the penis, for example, or the female organ for women; when there is no chi there, it is just a piece of flesh. Once the chi comes, the blood comes, and then how strong it is! But when the chi disappears, then even a beautiful woman or a handsome man in front of you cannot help you do anything. So basically, I wish you would learn what chi is. It is invisible and so volatile. Once you understand that, you will understand sex and why Taoists consider sex such a serious and important topic.

Sex has two categories. One is natural fulfillment and the other is mechanical performance. What is natural fulfillment? It is when you are not stimulated by a movie, image, or a story which makes you excited. When you are with a woman and are stirred with desire for her external beauty, this too is false desire. If you act on this, it is only mechanical performance, not the truth.

Natural fulfillment is the opposite. When you are resting in the middle of the night and your sexual member stirs naturally, then your energy is full. If you fulfill your natural sexual inclination, you will feel fine afterward because you have hurt nothing. If you do it on the right cyclic pattern, the energy will quickly restore itself.

Let me illustrate further. This example may not be the best choice but I do not have another good alternative. Opium originally was a medicine, now it is a popular drug. Opium gatherers need to get up at a certain time every morning to make a delicate cut in the skin of the opium fruit and wipe the resin from it. This process of gathering the opium is very gentle. If the plant is hurt, it will not produce any more resin. If you gather it at the wrong time or in the wrong way, the plant will die and you get no more resin. This is similar to your body and its sexual essence. Every morning it grows inside. If you take away the essence at the correct time, you will not hurt yourself and you can gather more for the next time.

Almost everybody would like to have more sex. Every time I ask my female patients if they are perhaps overdoing sex, they always say, "No! I never get enough!" Nobody says, "I really overdo it." They do not know that the body has limitations. It takes time for regeneration. The body also has cycles. When you are young, the Taoist books say you can do it maybe once a day. When you are a little older you can do it once every three days. In your middle years, maybe once a week. Then it becomes once every ten days, once a month, and so forth.

However, sexual capability depends on your personal physical condition. I wish for you to discover your own cycle, then wisely follow your cycle and you will not be hurt. If you have a natural sexual impulse and your partner is ready, then do it. If you are just stirred up by looking at external beauty or by food or drugs, then that is mechanical performance; there is no benefit to it, and if you overdo it, it becomes a hidden problem for your future health. If you are stirred up or full of energy and your partner is not ready, you are then presented with a good opportunity for your spiritual cultivation; that self-discipline and spiritual practice is one way to keep from having problems. Respecting the cycles in this way is also beneficial for your life and for the cultivation of immortality.

What I really want to share with you today is natural sex, the high Taoist spiritual sex. Natural sex is when the lower part is full and you do it without trouble. Mechanical performance is especially harmful to women. Women have many gynecological problems such as cancer of the uterus or cervix because they damaged themselves when they were not ready, not truly ready.

Before I go on to the next section for single people, I would like to mention briefly how both men and women can recycle their energy and restore their sexual potency.

I have an illustration in the first part of the *Book of Changes and the Unchanging Truth* that shows a human figure with a line down the front of the body and a line up the back. This is like the Yellow Route of the sun as it circles in the big sky. This circling in the body is the route the energy takes in our internal work. The refinement of self-cultivation is controlled by the mind, but the main principle is still naturalness. If someone uses the strength of his will power to make the circling go, then it is not beneficial, because the energy will strongly interfere. Naturalness in Taoist internal work is still the main thing. Only by the practice of the subtle mind can you bring about the integration. The will power is the determination and the subtle mind is the internal knowledge.

You must also follow the natural energy cycle in your daily practice. For instance, a good hour is just before the sun appears on the horizon. If you wish to lengthen your sexual manly power, get up early before the sun rises on the horizon. This is generally around 3 or 4 in the morning, so that you welcome the sunrise. Keep this up as a regular practice; your body will then naturally follow the same cycle. In this way, you will keep your manly energy longer. This is valuable knowledge explained by the ancient developed ones.

The recycling I have shown you of the front and back lines with the twelve houses of the zodiac is symbolic of the Yellow Route of the sun. Another practical cycle is that of the earth revolving to create day and night. Similarly, in our long life on earth, we have developed an internal physiological clock. Therefore, to stay in harmony with the natural cycles of the earth is the healthy way and the way to longevity.

Many of the achieved male and female Taoists I have known enjoyed a long life by living simply in a rural place. Their material goods and nutrition seem insufficient by modern standards, but they lived long and healthy lives without any serious problems. Since there were no hospitals then, all human beings needed to maintain their health in a natural way. They followed the natural life cycle that was built up through millions of years. The most important part of this pattern is rising early and enjoying the fresh air. They rise before sunrise and go to bed before or at sunset.

How can a man who is impotent cure himself? He can rise early, and when the sun is at about 25 - 45 degrees above the horizon, he faces the sun, inhales and swallows the sunshine nine times. There are some other instructions, but this is the main one. In this way, after three to six months, his impotence will be naturally cured and his sexual enjoyment will be naturally lengthened.

For a woman, when the moon is full, she faces the East and breathes in the moon energy six times. This can help with frigidity or sexual difficulties and maintain her youth.

You may wonder whether men may take the moon energy and woman may take the sun energy. Yes, especially if you are single, because a good human being has the inner balance of yin and yang. The purpose of yin/yang is to make the internal energy balance; that is why the intake of sun and moon energy is so valuable.

You might think that the moon is only a reflecting disc, and so how could it affect us? This question does not come from careful observation. For thousands of years we have known that the tides of the ocean are connected with the moon's cycle. We also know that women's menstrual cycles are connected with the moon. All living bodies are mostly water which is affected by the moon, so you can see its importance. Today we use rockets to go to the moon, but the real benefit of the moon in human life is being neglected, especially as it relates to individual life.

I also want to point out to you that the moon is closely connected to your emotional life. It is easy to lose your emotional balance during a full moon and become temporarily mad or crazy. It is even called lunacy. These things are obvious. They can be prevented by internal balance obtained by spiritual cultivation.

It takes time to remedy impotence, but if anyone utilizes the methods I have just given and combines them with breathing and herbs and acupuncture, it will naturally go away. It is so simple.

Now I wish to address the ones who are celibate and wish to have spiritual achievement. This is a more difficult situation for some than if you have a girlfriend or boyfriend. But some people, if they start very young, can follow this path. Other people can follow it after fulfilling their sexual desires, but they must stop their sexual activity early in life.

For women, it would be correct to stop in their thirties or forties.

If you do not have a strong sexual urge any more, then you can look for inner balance, because the human body itself is the integration of yin and yang. Your left side is yang and your right side is yin; the upper part of the body is yang; the lower part is yin. You can have harmony within yourself. You can cross the two opposite parts or sides of bodily energy and achieve integration. This is a safe way, but requires some good training. It is a high way and saves you a lot of trouble because you do not need to support another person emotionally or materially and you do not get involved in the emotional complications of a relationship; you only have yourself to look after.

A popular word today is "recycling." In the Integral Way, we practice recycling our sexual energy every day. Before the energy becomes a sexual fluid, you transform it into a kind of airy energy. If your water energy is too strong, you will have strong sexual desires and want to have a lot of sex. At the same time, the fiery energy in your head is irritable. There is another important principle from the *I Ching* and that is the balance of water energy and fire energy. If you feel angry, it means you have too much fire; if you have too much desire it means you are too watery. You are the manager and what you need to do is make the water and the fire change position so that the water energy comes to the upper part of the body and the fire energy comes down to the lower part of the body. This creates an image of cooking, with the water on top and the fire underneath. If you get it cooking well, then you will have good regeneration of your energy and can maintain your health and lengthen your years. This is the preliminary practice to further spiritual achievement.

Q: How do we go about this exchange of fire and water and how do we have sex with ourselves and recycle the energy?

Master Ni: Through energy guidance in Taoist exercises, breathing, internal work and diet. The purpose of all of these is to balance yourself. Stay away from bad books or movies; they will make you watery. If you read spiritual books, the water energy will subtly transform and be distributed to all parts of your body evenly. This is the best way to start to transform your water energy.

Q: Even if one is not celibate, is it still beneficial to keep balanced with the fire at the bottom and water at the top?

Master Ni: You are absolutely right. At another level, I would say that as long as you are not doing intensive cultivation, then it is still safe to have sexual relationships and maintain a certain level of balance. Nature itself will usually adjust things. It is a difficult path to try to do cultivation and still have sexual relationships.

Even though you spend a lot of time hunting around for a sexual partner, you still need to fulfill your own spiritual purpose. In the Integral Way, we still make single cultivation the basic training and sexual cultivation something extraordinary. You need special training and preparation to do that.

Q: You mentioned having intercourse between the upper and lower parts of the body, how about left with right?

Master Ni: Very simple. Hold your hands together, cross your legs, and focus your eyes on the tip of your nose. You have fulfilled the intercourse of the right and the left sides' energy.

Q: Earlier you said something about women utilizing the moon's energy. Did this apply to women who are celibate?

Master Ni: Yes. However, in your case, because you are celibate, spend more time with the early sun and not so much with the moon because it is already too strong in you. Once you have more yang energy directly from the male source, the sun, then you will feel much more balanced.

I tell my female Taoist friends that just because they are not married does not mean that they do not have a husband; the great sun is their husband. I also tell my single male Taoists not to think they have no wife; the moon is their wife. It all depends on how you use the perfect yin and perfect yang energy to balance yourself.

Q: I know of some spiritual groups today who teach celibacy as the highest path, but in reality they have a secret sexual practice. Is there any sound spiritual reason for guarding the fact that those practices exist? I notice that Taoism does not hide the fact of sexual practices at all, but it does guard the spiritual knowledge involved. Is this true?

Master Ni: Yes, that is true. There are two things that we guard most carefully. One is how you utilize sexual energy from other human beings so that you are benefitted without harming them. The other is how to communicate and relate to spiritual beings as freely as you would to friends in the physical sphere. Those two things are sacred secrets to us, even though they both can be omitted in spiritual achievement.

The teachers who led their students to practice celibacy but had a secret sexual practice themselves did so perhaps out of good intentions. At least I would hope so. It is like adults who drink wine or coffee but do not let the children do it. They think that they know better but they do not have the strength to resist any more. They have not totally lost their vision about it being poison, so they prohibit the children from doing it.

I said at another time that most religious paths include one bad principle. That is, if people sometimes fall down when walking (to them, to walk with two legs means to have a sexual relationship), they insist everyone jump on one leg (this means to live singly without sexual relationship)! Worldly life and relationships, especially relationships between men and women, cause pain, disappointment, sorrow and misery. One way people express their extreme attitude about relationship is theatrically to sever conjugal life, but they still engage in it secretly.

It is not contradictory to see that some spiritual traditions are still having an inner struggle. Their teachings are put too high and their actions are low. The leaders have learned from their own religion and have also inherited this struggle from the past generations of their religion. Some religious teachers say very seriously, "Women are poison, gold is poison, stay away." To a Taoist, it could be poison, but it could also be a great, great gift.

Celibacy with a special and creative purpose in life deserves respect. Many high achievements were accomplished by those who concentrated on a single goal and channeled their energy into work or art or practice rather than other things. Celibacy also has a health value when properly managed. There are many stages and situations in life which are simply not suitable to sexual activity or involvement. On the spiritual path, however, the true value is internal harmony and balance. It does not lie in any concept such as "Celibacy." Celibacy holds no superiority over any other style of life in spiritual practice.

Many other things are more valuable than having fun and having sex. There are higher levels of having fun, such as Taoist "internal sex" and other methods which reach for different high spiritual pleasures.

That is the conclusion of the second talk.

For this third talk, let us answer the questions of the people here.

Q: What is the Taoist view on the purpose of sex?

Master Ni: Such a big topic! Generally speaking, we are born to be distinguished as yang or yin, man or woman. If you do not fulfill your sex at a certain age in your life, you will feel incomplete in some way. So at some time, at a certain stage of your life, you must do it. You must achieve internal and external harmony; this is the purpose of sex.

You may also ask, is the purpose of Taoist sex to continue your life through your children? It depends. In the *Tao Teh Ching*, it says that once you complete your big task, you withdraw yourself. Suppose you are a farmer and have a big piece of land. If you do not have a child, who will continue to make the land useful? But once you complete your task, you withdraw.

Women over forty, or after they give birth to a child, are not strongly supported by the general vital energy any more. So what should they do? They should cultivate themselves and look more towards spiritual achievement. But today, women over forty use hormones or other things to make them more sexually responsive; even so, it is not the same as before they were forty. There is a natural way in Taoist medicine to lengthen the age of women with herbs so they can continue to be sexually active, but this is not an external thing. Spiritual students should make their companionship more spiritually enjoyable, and less physical. I know this is difficult in today's world.

Q: Are you saying that women should naturally stop sex after forty?

Master Ni: If they have a spiritual purpose. Men do not stop at forty, they stop much later. Why is the sex life of women so short? Women's bodies bear a much greater burden in having and raising children then men's do, for one thing. And on top of that, many women today work in addition to their responsibilities as a wife and mother. By the time a woman has reached her forties she has expended a great deal of her energy in life, and she could greatly benefit spiritually by directing it into cultivation at that age rather than by continuing to pursue sexual activity. The same could be said of men as they work to satisfy their job-related ambitions. Cultivation will renew the energy. Sex will only deplete it further. Many women at this age have lost much of their natural sexual drive and energy, so if they use something external, some kind of lubrication, then sex becomes a mechanical performance done out of psychological or emotional need. It is not physically beneficial, it is only habitual behavior.

In the Integral Way, remember one thing. In general, we do not appreciate the single life. We appreciate mutually supportive relationships. If a couple wishes to do single cultivation they can use separate rooms and then at the right time, reunion happens. By living together with general personal energy contact, unconsciously, subtly, the yin and yang energies of the couple are still harmonized. The two people need spiritual understanding, the same spiritual goal and spiritual cultivation to support such pure harmony without emotional competition or physical abuse for each other.

Q: Master Ni, today homosexuality is becoming more and more common, which means yin with yin and yang with yang essentially. What is your view of this kind of sexual behavior? Is it damaging?

Master Ni: You can see that even if two men or two women are together, one is more feminine and one is more masculine. Thus we can still put them in yin/yang categories because one must perform the yin function and one must perform the yang. They may have had some kind of bad experience with the opposite sex which made them turn away. But human behavior cannot be decided by one rigid rule. From my understanding, homosexuality is not as energetically supportive as the union of a true man and a true woman. But you see, even a real man and woman sometimes have difficulty being a real man and real woman. Most people take personality supplements from other people they meet. A healthy, broad-minded person will enjoy all kinds of personalities, whether inclined to yin or to yang. In true sexual performance, however, the togetherness of yin and yang is the correct model, but homosexuality is just a circumstance.

Q: How does one go about choosing the right sexual partner? Should there be a certain kind of relationship? A lot of times people have sex and they're just friends. Is there a right kind of emotional bond that should exist between the two partners?

Master Ni: There is one important principle in Taoist sexual performance; if there is no love, then no sex. There must be true love, then there is true energy communication.

Sometimes you may have true love, but the other partner does not physically or mentally respond; then you must stop. If you go ahead, it is the same as masturbation - a solo.

As this subject pertains to marriage, you may read the commentary on marriage in my work, the *Book of Changes and the Unchanging Truth.*

Q: Why is the reproductive vitality of women more short-lived than that of men, and does this mean that spiritual achievement is also limited for them?

Master Ni: No, definitely not. At the spiritual level, men and women are equal. As a matter of fact, women are sometimes more sensitive to spiritual knowledge because men are more aggressive and coarse minded. As to why women's sexual life is shorter, it is just a natural, physical fact. But I tell you this, some women, if they know how to cultivate themselves, can enjoy longer sexual health, comparatively, without using drugs.

If you are young, and you have interest in spiritual cultivation, do not wait until you are old. Now that your breasts are still full and your organs are still moist, it is good time to seriously do spiritual sublimation instead of still depending on that part of a man to satisfy your desires. I think it is a waste.

Q: What are the most favorable positions for healthy sex?

Master Ni: For healthy sex, the positions are changeable. No one position is best. The most favorable position is the woman on top and the man beneath so that you can let the woman be the active partner. The *Tao Teh Ching* teaches the man to follow the feminine principle because men are always burning with energy and wish to hurry up and finish it. When you finish, the woman is not through yet. So you should let the woman be on top and have the active role in this business. You just accommodate the activity, and just respond to the flow. This is Taoist sex which you can discover from the *I Ching*, or the *Tao Teh Ching*, not only with regard to position but how to do sex. The woman should be the man, and the man should be the woman in sexual matters.

Q: What is the best position for sex when the couple stays still?

Master Ni: Sitting face to face. The man needs two pillows to elevate him so that not too much weight is put on the woman's leg. I will talk about it later.

There are many postures. Mostly, different postures are for different purpose, not serious cultivation. They are not recommended Taoist practice. There are only two recommended practices. One is sitting together and holding each other. The other way is to do "canoeing": the woman can have a little more action on top and the man can lay down with face up. That position is called canoeing because the ancient canoes were round like logs. Thus, the woman straddles the man. This is a Taoist posture for sexual energy adjustment. By using the canoeing posture, the man can also learn how to control himself without expressing animal impulse in all aspects of life.

Q: Are there positions in sex that are harmful?

Master Ni: All positions are harmful if it is a mechanical performance.

Q: For Western style sex, how long should the sex act be? How long in the Taoist technique?

Master Ni: If the woman has one orgasm, I think you should stop. If she wants to have more orgasms, you should not let her do it if you truly love her and do not want to see her work ineffectively in the next couple of days and grow old so fast.

You ask about the Taoist practice. It depends on the performance. It could be the whole seven days, if you use the right position. But if your chi is not there, you cannot do it. Truthfully speaking, sexual performance is a spiritual cultivation. If you mind thinks of anything else, then your organ cannot stay inside the vagina; it will shrink. Only if you are there without your mind taking your energy away, then you can be together. Once your mind withdraws even a little, the performance is done; there is nothing there. Do you understand? This is why I call it a spiritual cultivation.

So you ask how long. This is the practice of mind and spirit, not just the sexual organs, because the sexual organs will separate if you are wandering mentally or spiritually. If the woman's interest goes away, then there is only a piece of flesh, there is no benefit any more.

Q: Are you saying that in the case of both men and women, the more frequently you have sex, the more rapidly you age?

Master Ni: Both ways. If you have sex not according to your own physical cycle, you will get older faster. If it is the right time and you do not do it, your anxiety and tension will make you older faster unless you have already truly achieved yourself spiritually. It is the same thing, no benefit.

Q: Generally speaking, what is the best time of the month for a woman to have sex? And also the best time of the day?

Master Ni: For a woman, the best time is before and after menstruation, because the energy is coming down and it is much easier to reach orgasm. At other times you have to make a lot of effort to gather all the energy from the other parts of the body, and even then sometimes you cannot make it happen. During menstruation, you like to do it then also. Why? The energy is already full and falls to that part. But if the bleeding is too strong, then do not do it because it could cause an unhealthy condition for the organs of both sexes, especially the woman.

Q: Master Ni, did you say that you should stop after the woman has one orgasm?

Master Ni: Good sex is a mutually high enjoyment. You make everything ready. Let the woman start. If she has one orgasm, then let her have her choice. Sometimes she wants two, so let her have two. If a woman is strong and you are seldom together and she wants three, then let her have three. But still, do not do too much. You can use another position that is similar to a tantric practice where you sit up together holding each other. You are still enjoying the same good feeling without looking for further orgasms.

Q: How about men?

Master Ni: I do not think men should have orgasms.

Q: At all?

Master Ni: Occasionally. As I said earlier, it would depend on their age. For men before sixty, maybe one ejaculation a month or every 45 days would be safe.

Q: How do you control the urge to release the chi, or have the orgasm? Should you develop skills in withstanding that pressure? How do you know when to have orgasm?

Master Ni: If sex is based on tension that you want to release, then you can never control it. It comes like a thousand horses suddenly rushing out of a burning stable. You could never stop it. So for men, first learn how to calm yourself down, how to discipline yourself. What is the hurry? Where are you going? Calm down. If there is tension, there will be release but no enjoyment.

The best time of day is when you are relaxed and rested enough. If you are not relaxed and you do not have energy because you are distracted by work or worry, or anything else, and you do sex, then it is a mechanical performance. When you are hungry, you eat. When you are thirsty, you drink. That is natural fulfillment. If you eat when you are not hungry or drink when you are not thirsty, it is called mechanical performance. Do your best to keep away from it but fulfill, if you like, the natural function. The best time of day, therefore, is anytime when you are relaxed.

Also, do not participate in group sex. There is no benefit at all. It is not general human behavior. If you do it, you will still have tension because there are always others to stimulate you.

Q: Are orgasms healthy for woman?

Master Ni: Sometimes a woman will have a bad temper. Orgasm is a cure for them. If they do not have orgasms, they are like a cat with a burning tail. They will bite anything around them. But I do not exhaust yourself with orgasms. It will make you older faster and wear your organs out sooner. You cannot stay young.

When you are really ready and the time is right, orgasm comes so easily. That is natural performance. You can tell that yourself. Then once you have the orgasm, you can change positions. Then what follows can be a cultivation. The energy will regenerate and you nurture and benefit each other. Only one part of yourself are you releasing. This is a good balanced way to do it.

Q: Master Ni, when you said that a man should have an orgasm once a week or once a month, and to limit your sexual activity to your natural cycle, does a man who does not have an orgasm still lose energy by having sexual relations?

Master Ni: It depends. To a spiritual person, no orgasm or ejaculation is a basic discipline. If you lose it, you lose the battle at the beginning. It is difficult to re-start after that. But if a man, because he has the control through T'ai Chi or breathing exercise, can master this, he can enjoy long sex without ejaculation. This is a special capability which ordinary people do not have.

I still suggest that you limit orgasms. Why? It is something when a man is still going strong in his 40's or 50's, but how about still going strong in your 80's and 90's? I suggest you adopt the psychology of a marathon runner rather than a sprinter. If you have the capability and the right partner, you will be a man rich in energy and will naturally like to spend more time at it. But you ask me, is it still a loss of energy? It is. If you have nothing else to do, you can do it. If you wish to accumulate subtle energy, then you may like to move on to another level.

Q: Is there an invocation that can be used during or after sex?

Master Ni: There is a ritual and invocation which can make you ready for sex, and then a ritual for energy restoration afterwards. The invocation and simple description of the natural ritual is in the *Workbook for Spiritual Development.*

Q: What is the proper way to gather energy after sex?

Master Ni: There are two ways to do it. One way is doing dao-in exercise; that can easily be learned. Another way is that often before people have sex, they drink wine, and then go to bed and have sex. That is not correct. Drink a good herb wine or tonic herbal tea after sex, not before.

If anyone loses energy during sex, especially men, drink one raw egg stirred up in a cup with a little good wine and a small amount of brown sugar, but not too much. This will compensate for what you lost. For women, it is the same. Some people cannot have sugar. For them there is something else - good Chinese herbal tea.

Q: How can we know the "bad energy" days on which to avoid sex?

Master Ni: This is more complicated. Do not do it on a night of no moon. I have already explained this in the first part of my book, the *Book of Changes and the Unchanging Truth.* In general, a bad energy day is when there is a big wind, with a storm and thunder. This is not the right time to have sex. If you are mentally disturbed, do not do sex then either.

Q: Do Taoists approve of oral sex, and if so, for what purpose?

Master Ni: As a whole, I approve of natural sex as I have so far described: to do it with your sexual organs. Oral sex is out of a transformed unfulfilled desire from your childhood and a habit.

Q: What foods increase or decrease sexual desire? Are there any foods that are good to eat afterwards?

Master Ni: I explained this in my talks on diet, which you can read later. After sex, warm food and drink are good, but not before. Do not eat ice cream afterwards. Eating bad food afterwards or before can cause ulcers.

Q: At what point in a relationship or friendship does sex become appropriate? Should one not have sex until a strong emotional bond has first developed?

Master Ni: I think I answered that. No love, no sex. This is an important principle of mutual energy support in the Integral Way.

Q: What about sexual activity that does not result in actual intercourse, but involves kissing and touching. What is your feeling on that? If you were trying to cultivate spiritually and were trying not to have sexual relationships but you find yourself being with someone sexually, is it wrong to stop short of actual intercourse?

Master Ni: This is an interesting topic. It really relates back to celibacy. If you have been cultivating your energy and it is primarily self-centered, then even by touching hands or looking into someone's eyes your sexual needs will be stimulated. If your energy is dull, such things will not interest you, but if you wish to go over the line and have sex, it changes everything that you originally expected from yourself.

This question is from a woman. There are several considerations. One is that if you engage in behavior which is sexually stimulating to men, such as kissing and hugging, and then refuse or back down from intercourse, this is usually considered teasing behavior. Men do not like this, so at the social level it is not suggested.

Second, even if you have a partner who agrees ahead of time, few couples can do this often without building up their desire and causing an extreme congestion of energy in the abdomen. The result is usually intercourse. Do not be too idealistic.

Third, if your desire is strong, you might consider the alternative of doing Taoist sex occasionally for the purpose of energy adjustment.

Fourth, some women have a strong emotional need for affection as expressed by kissing and hugging. If you are serious about celibacy and cultivation and if you work on keeping your mind under control and avoid things like romantic movies and being in places where there are lots of couples, your emotional desire will lessen. Fulfillment in other areas of your life such as female friendships and stimulating work will also lessen the emotional needs.

Q: You said where there is no love, there should be no sex. Well, how many people can a person love at any one time? How deep need the love be? Is "like" okay?

Master Ni: This is important. If it is a partner that you "like," it means that it is on the sexual level. If it is a partner that you "love" and "respect," it is on the spiritual level. Generally, sex without deep love occurs frequently. If you wish to make love with some special person for spiritual benefit, then follow the guideline of no love - no sex. There is no benefit in sex without love because your soul is not kindled. Spiritual fulfillment is different from physical fulfillment. Sex with many different partners is physical fulfillment. Spiritually beneficial opportunities are much harder to find. Generally, when you find someone to sleep with, your souls do not embrace each other; you may share the same room but you have different dreams.

Q: Is it possible to love more than one person at one time? Is it healthy to love three people and make love with all three?

Master Ni: Love has no boundaries. In following the Integral Way, you are not allowed to become attached to only one beauty because if you are so attached, you can hardly achieve spiritually. You do not lose yourself in love, you do not harm the other in love, and you maintain your own spiritual center.

As to the core of your question, in real life, people may do it. Spiritual guidance teaches us not to extend ourselves in that area or any area of physical life. Our definitions of the words "natural" and "original" mean the balanced nature of all three spheres of love. Obviously, it is not encouraged to have fun in sexual matters without mental and spiritual consideration. When I say no love, no sex, the word "love" may differ from the way that general people define it. It is an achievement to know what to love and how to love. It is knowledge. It has been a secret. Why is it a secret? Because different teachers from the same cultural background teach differently. The ancient Taoists were said to have relationships with different partners in different stages of life. In the more formal teaching it was just as I said: rarify your desire. It particularly points at sexual interest. The direction is right, but how much, or the amount of rarification, is individual. There was a standard established according to different ages. I think it is a generalization and has no definite value. I do not even relate that standard to modern people.

Someone said that the Yellow Emperor had slept with 1,200 virgins and thus at last he rode on a yellow dragon and flew to his Heavenly palace. Many men have that type of fantasy. However, China has been a monarchy since then and all the emperors had lots of women. And all of them died young, at an average age of 30 or 40. There were only two emperors who lived longer than their eighties because they kept away from having too much sex. From this fact, you know the way of balance is a safety bar that keeps you from danger. Surely, there is special Taoist knowledge about beneficial sex. As I have mentioned, it is a secret knowledge of what to love and how to love. Thus, it is an achievement. If it is an achievement, then it can be known after your achievement. You might think you want to know about it. However, if you know about it but you cannot realize it in your life, it is of no benefit. Thus, the way of balance is the broad truth that almost everybody can apply in their lives.

Q: I find that having sex without having an orgasm dries the semen up. Is that healthy?

Master Ni: The purpose of Taoist sex is not to dry your semen up, but to transfer it and also to stabilize your mind. People only become dried up from mechanical sex that drains the energy from other parts of the body. It is not a matter of being dry, it is a matter of not being gathered.

Q: Is there a difference, in Taoist terms, between a physical ejaculation and total orgasm? Can there be one without the other?

Master Ni: Yes. In the Integral Way we value internal intercourse, which means you have the happy feeling inside your own body. In this practice you break up all the blockages in the muscle system, the nervous system and all the various systems of the body. Internal orgasm is highly important in true immortal practice.

There are two special terms for male and female energy; actually, they are flexible and can be used for either men or women. Mercury, we say, represents the volatile changeable watery energy and it needs the energy of lead, the heavy, steady energy, to stabilize it. Mercury represents the semen of the man and lead represents the female sexual energy in the fluid. If a man is without a woman and practices celibacy, and even if he practices a mental discipline, he will still have night trouble and involuntary ejaculation. There is no benefit in this. Women who are celibate also have involuntary orgasms during their sleep. This is because if your energy is too strong or too heavy, you need the opposite energy to balance it. If you do not want to know how to utilize this principle, you are just being superstitious and idealistic.

Many people are put into mental hospitals. Some of them suffer from psychological problems and others just do not have good sexual relationships or good sexual performance; thus they become crazy from their mercury energy. It happens to both men and women. So in the Integral Way, men and women need each other to be the "lead" energy to stabilize their own "mercury" energy. Men's and women's energies connect just like mercury and lead. Even if you do not have sex, it is still good to live together because just that feeling can stabilize your unstable "mercury" energy.

Q: What is a good form of exercise for women to do that would enhance their sexuality?

Master Ni: At this point, I would like to express my observation about modern women. They go to gyms and train their muscles, they jog along the highways and they build themselves up to be as strong as men. Schools are coeducational and men and women share all kinds of sports and athletics. Physical distinctions between the sexes are beginning to disappear. This has come about through the negligence of some leaders of modern education. If a woman becomes too strong, where is she going to find a good man? Who can she find to be her happy companion sexually? She will naturally be disappointed in the physical condition of men and complain about their weakness. Women are already resorting to masturbation with strong vibrators or rubber penises instead of the natural organ of a man. If women become too strong, they cannot appreciate or respect men for their manly performance any more, and that is sad.

Leaders of education do not know anything about this; they only try to make women as strong as men for economic purposes. If the focus were on a natural life, they would see that something is obviously wrong with all of this. Surely today's women can easily be leaders in all areas of human activity, but it is difficult for them to enjoy the natural happiness of being truly feminine. I am not saying we should stop women from becoming physically strong, but I look at it from the point of view of sexual enjoyment and happiness.

To respond to your question, I recommend T'ai Chi movement, light stretching and some swimming for enjoyment and not for racing purpose, and some good dancing too. Housework is good exercise as well. All these things will help you enjoy the naturalness of your physical condition and improve it also. T'ai Chi movement was originally a martial art, but I am not advising you take it to that level. If you were to do that, you would build yourself differently.

The second important recommendation is to stop using tampons during menstruation because although they cleanse the blood, they suck your energy from the organ. Use some other method. I make this recommendation to all my Taoist women friends.

Q: Master Ni, I have one last question. You said no love, no sex. I am having a problem with that. What is true love? If it is not something we experience in everyday life, then we would end up not having sex for most of our life?

Master Ni: It seems that it is difficult for you to love someone. For me, it is so easy. I love almost all the cuties.

Taoist sexual fulfillment is not a matter of physical temptation on one side or on both sides. There must be spiritual harmony between the couple. The thoughts in a man's or woman's mind, "Do I love this person or like this person?" are subjective. You need to know that your partner has a similar interest in you as you do in her or him. It is the openness of the partner and one's own sincerity that brings about spiritual harmony. Sex is only one expression of spiritual harmony. Spiritual harmony is the high point of all relationships.

There was a student of philosophy who had spent all of his life energy attending classes, studying, writing, and discussing ideological and philosophical issues. In his thirties, he had his first girlfriend at a hot-springs resort. This is what he said to a friend: "At last I found the highest wisdom that I never discovered in those cold, thick philosophical books I have always read. I have finally found the true philosophy and it is so simple."

My friend, true love is true life. Such a thing can never be realized by the ideological or mythological development of the mind. When the ideological and mythological complication is dissolved, true beauty and love is seen by the simplicity of the mind. Thus, set about attaining that kind of simple but pertinent mind first. There's no point to sitting and discussing it because the real thing is simpler than what the mind thinks about most of the time.

The next part is a new discussion on this topic.

Q: Master Ni, would you give us the secret of Taoist dual cultivation, at the level you feel is right to tell?

Master Ni: Many people use dual cultivation as transfigured sex. For them, it is just another way of doing sex. If that is the case, it is a psychological issue not a spiritual purpose. The spiritual purpose of dual cultivation is for internal adjustment and harmony. If the partner is right, it is beneficial to both sides.

Some basic principles should be known. For women, before and after menstruation and before and after ovulation are difficult times, but they are suitable times for doing dual cultivation.

Also, a man of no cultivation or special achievement usually has an ejaculation. Ejaculation can cause the woman to have another disaster; a pregnancy without purpose or preparation. So therefore, a man should be trained. The man should have a full erection. He can check out the erection; the dragon (penis) should be warm; in Taoist terms it is called the fiery dragon. At the tip, the mouth of the dragon should not secrete any liquid at all during the time it is applied. That is the standard.

For the woman, the usual requirement in dual cultivation is never having given birth to a child. If she has given birth to a child, there are two ways. I recommend the natural way, which is the using of herbs; and the other special way makes the muscle of the vagina come back to normal by plastic surgery.

So the applied situation is to do it at the right time. Usually dual cultivation is for spiritual purpose. You have seen the tai chi diagram; it is a man holding a woman and a woman holding a man in a sitting position. That is one secret we did not tell before. When both are sitting, it is important that it be 90% mental and spiritual discipline. Why? Usually a typical man and woman, when they have sex, engage in a form of fighting: you kill me, I kill you. More accurately and truthfully, it is not you kill me and I kill you, it is each person wishes to kill themselves by the friction, aggressiveness and brutal action. They try to make a fast finish, to reach the highest point. If they are looking for orgasm, it is soon over. By so doing, spiritually, it indicates that the following days at work will be hard and making business deals will be difficult.

Dual cultivation in general is for a spiritual purpose, to eliminate necessitating such hard work or difficult deals. It is for adjustment and it has several levels. One passive level is for physical adjustment; the man and woman are in the suitable age range and need some adaptation. Otherwise, their psychology and emotional match would be bad. For the high level of spiritual function, usually it is a younger woman and older man who need that support. The complete union is on three levels, but I do not need to describe it deeply. You know the benefit and the principle.

When you sit together, there is a certain inter-operating of the energy. Some traditions teach you to use mantras. Mantras are for preparation. There are two things that are important; one is breathing. The man's breath and the woman's breath are both different energies and contain different hormones; so during that time, when the woman inhales, the man exhales.

The other important adjustment during sexual energy cultivation is the orbit circulation. The circulation is a complete course through two people, as the tai chi diagram shows. The man and woman cooperate with that internal energy movement after the harmonization of energy comes to a correct stage. Usually it comes up from the organs through the man's spinal bone, through the head and comes down through the tongue. Then it goes through the woman, from the head downward to the spinal bone. Usually it is done clockwise, but it also can be done counterclockwise. This cooperation needs some practice. If both come to full energy, the light can be seen - different auras, different lights. They do the movement with conscious control; it is not just imagination or the practice of visualization, a real light can be amassed and emitted. Generally speaking, a man and a woman do nothing, just hold each other and let nature take care of itself.

When your energy is full, it is suitable to do that. If both energies are weak, it cannot be done; it is not beneficial. That would be employing the wild imagination and is of no use.

There is another important secret. If dual cultivation or partner is beneficial for you, usually you will know in your heart, but during the cultivation, you still can open your eyes a little bit and see. If your eyes have a little gentle fog or mist it means the energy is coming through; it may be different colors, usually white. What I talk about is the hard part of dual cultivation; the choice of partner is more important.

Primarily I approve of the Taoist way of sexual performance that is man on bottom, woman on top, just like the hexagram Tai, with the earth on top and Heaven on the bottom. In that way, the man will not damage the woman. The woman knows how to handle her own organ. So the man follows the teaching of the *Tao Teh Ching* and the woman can be as active as the average aggressive man. It has one benefit. Sometimes women have sexual organ problems because of slight damage occurring when they have sex: their sexual energy is not full enough or the man is too aggressive and rough. Only the woman is sensitive enough to manage herself to avoid a creating future physical problems in that area. Cancer can start from such small damage. That is the second level.

The third level is sitting dual cultivation as in a complete tai chi diagram. Both man and woman follow the principle of the *Tao Teh Ching*; doing by non-doing; making love by non-making.

The top level that my tradition respects, is a man and a woman living together, maybe even in one room, but no overt sexual activity. In reality, it is a kind of harmony or natural energy blending. If the energy harmony exists, it is excellent. So if you talk about the secret of the shiens, this is the final secret. I give almost all of it to you. See that you achieve it wisely; that you apply it to the right partner in the right way.

Q: Master Ni, what is the other thing we should pay attention to when we have all four levels of love making?

Master Ni: The external conditions of dual cultivation pertain to all levels. It should be done in a good environment, not during a storm and not in a disturbed or noisy place. That is not suitable or beneficial. Drinking or taking drugs is terrible and should be avoided, even in general life.

In general, for protection of their health, young people need to have more sexual discipline and not overuse their sexual organs or sexual essence. In that way, they can live longer. For young people, even with a vegetable diet, there is still some stimulation. Garlic, Chinese leeks and the seeds of Chinese leeks, for example, are strong sexual foods. Many of these things are suitable to help older people with insufficient sexual function. I do not mean they need them for a sexual purpose, however. Usually young people generate enough sexual energy each day by themselves but older people need all kinds of help. This is the correct utilization of Taoist knowledge. The Taoist culture is proud about knowing many foods and herbs that can help one's sexual energy. Even the dead male silkworm can rejuvenate male sexual energy, but not female sexual energy. Female sexual energy has different herb formulas.

If young people are really serious about sexual discipline, being vegetarian will help, but they will still have sexual desire. However, it is better to moderate oneself with a selective diet. The cultivation and skills for self-maintenance can be learned from my other books. Our human systems are quite delicate; each thing affects the entire being.

If you are serious about vegetarianism, there are four directions: vegetables, fruits, nuts and grains. Vegetables are divided into three categories: roots, leafy vegetables and beans. All of these need to be balanced. A variety or balance of the four foods can usually sustain a life quite well and natural herbs can be a useful addition if they are not overly concentrated. I do not suggest that older people stop eating good meat, but I do not support people directly killing. Killing has a different energy; it does not serve any spiritual benefit to learn killing.

Q: Master Ni, this is my personal experience. For people who are seeking a mutually beneficial long term relationship together for spiritual purposes, communication with regard to sex is important. Needless to say, it is often difficult because sex can be an emotional issue and because sex performance is related to so many different things. If a couple cannot talk to each other directly, then perhaps some other form of communication can be made, such as writing. Sometimes writing is better because verbal communication is mostly impulsive, unclear and difficult.

A couple who came to me for counseling over a period of years were not sharing the type of sexual intimacy and pleasure that both were capable of. Why not? Poor communication. They went back and forth from wanting to be celibate, to having sex, to wanting other lovers, when really what the two people wanted was a harmonious and balanced relationship together. Clear communication between the two people about their needs and wants was needed. They did it by writing "love letters" to each other. Once they resolved a few basic misunderstandings, they were able to communicate clearly, lovingly and be expressive and intimate. Their sexual communication was greatly improved and enhanced. However, even if they had decided to stay celibate, the communication enhanced their emotional, mental and spiritual harmony. What do you think of this?

Master Ni: This is an example of real life between two people who live under one same roof. Sometimes emotional difficulty is experienced even if there is truly no involvement by one person with an outside party such as another lover. To allow the situation to improve, there needs to be sufficient tolerance and wait for the temporary misunderstanding to go away by itself. At a heart level, people can more easily accommodate each other than at a mind level. In real life, especially when considering how to treat others, it is better to let the heart have dominion than to let the mind play out its unsettled nature caused by its own immaturity.

Chapter 6

The Principle of Internal and External Harmony

The interpretation made by the *I Ching* illustrates the traditional secret of immortality and natural harmony. It is a principle to be applied within and without.

Pure yang ☰ and pure yin ☷ are the distinctive symbols of pure spiritual and material energy; things and events in the practical world are expressed as formations of these two combined energies, no single element performs by itself. Therefore it is also said that there is yin in yang and yang in yin at the depth of all realities, things and events, simple or complicated.

These two basics, yang and yin, form the fundamental energy patterns. The yang group ☰ uses ☳ , ☵ and ☶ to express the strong, the middle and the lesser yang energy by the position of ⚊. They show the depth yang reaches: the strong one reaches the bottom ☳, the middle reaches the middle ☵ , and the lesser reaches the surface ☶ . The yin group ☷ uses ☴, ☲ and ☱ to express the strong, the middle and the lesser yin energy ⚋. They show the depth yin reaches; the strong one reaches the bottom ☴ , the middle reaches the middle ☲ and the lesser reaches the surface ☱.

The above is basic. When this symbolic system is applied to spiritual cultivation as discussed in *The Story of Two Kingdoms*, the two groups of symbols express themselves differently: among the six spiritual elements, shen, or spirit, is represented by ☲ which is yin in the big category, while tsing or sexual impetus is represented by ☵ which is yang in the big category. Here, "big category" means generally categorized or in the broad sense, not for specific use. There, in *The Story of Two Kingdoms*, yang and yin are reversed.

Sexual energy is the vital chi and when it transforms into watery or fluid form, we use the symbol ☵ for water to express it. Spiritual energy is vital chi; when it transforms into fiery or motivating form, we use the symbol ☲ for fire to express it. Traditionally, ☵ is also used to express the moon and po, which are the typical examples of yin energy. ☲ is also used to express the sun and hun which are typical examples of yang energy. ☵ and ☲ are opposites because it is believed that the sun has yin energy as its essence and the moon has yang energy as its essence.

All lives on earth are the result of the interplay of the fire and water energies. Lives on earth are expressions of one stage of the integration that produces shaped and formed life. Nobody has, so far, lived longer than the sun or the moon. The next stage of spiritual evolution is that of becoming totally spiritualized. For the male foundation as ☲ the sun, its middle line is exchanged with the female moon. With the addition of the ☵ as its middle line —, yang restores its purity to become ☰, and yin restores its purity to become ☷. The same thing happens when the moon accepts the middle line from the sun. For further knowledge, continue to study my books, this one in particular. Do not be confused by the metaphysical use of spiritual language. One must be flexible when applying the trigrams to different situations; the definitions as they are presented in the *I Ching* must not be rigidly adhered to.

In immortal practice, the secret lies in reversion. As Chapter 40 of the *Tao Teh Ching* says: "Reversion is the direction toward which Tao moves, and softness is the application that Tao tends to foster." Because the natural tendencies of yang and yin have interchanged, the secret is in the convergence of both patterns of energy. Yang in general means active energy. Yin in general describes receptive and responsive energy. When, in spiritual integration, the yang energy lowers itself to the acceptance of the yin, and allows the more stable or steady yin energy to stabilize the union, this is traditionally termed as the interchange of the host and the guest.

In an ordinary relationship, usually the male acts the role of initiator and the female expresses the role of passive acceptance. With the purpose of ☲, the spirits take the lost middle — line in order to restore the purity of universal male energy. Thus, in dual cultivation, the roles of man and woman are exchanged. Single cultivation usually refers to dual cultivation to illustrate the reversed order, using the ecstacy of a couple in the act of making love; the three pairs of internal energies "make love" to each other to sustain the durability of the union.

Because a life is the convergence of all kinds of energies and spirits, death means the scatteredness of the composed life. Longevity is the result of holding together all energies and spirits while spiritual immortality is holding together all the spirits.

The yin-yang polarities of the eight trigrams in the "Internal Mysterious Marriage" arrangement suggests the practice. Its explanation is on page 7 of *The Story of Two Kingdoms*. It does not imply a definite classification. If it did, you would not be able to find coherence in both the pre-Heaven and post-Heaven arrangement.

The general knowledge is that high achievement is the integration of six elements: hun ☳ and po ☱ (which are both human spirits, but their natures are opposite) as a pair of yin and yang; tsing (physical essence) ☵ and sen (spiritual essence) ☲, another pair of yin and yang; consciousness and intent ☴ and will ☶ as another pair of yin and yang. The first three, ☳, ☵ and ☶ fall into the yang ☰ category and the other three, ☱, ☲ and ☴ fall into the yin ☷ category.

In each circumstance, yin ☷ indicates the physical foundation of each symbol; it expresses the self-centered concepts which stubbornly associate with worldly life and which are a part of each element. Total achievement comes from success in eliminating all yin influence from each of the six levels, until one's new spiritual life becomes complete as total yang energy ☰. The reversion makes the immortal practice.

Harmony or Perfect Marriage or Relationship

Above: Yin
(Female Energy On Top)

A young man chooses a more mature woman to receive help. See Hexagram 53, Jen

Accomplishment happens by correct order. See Hexagram 63, Chi Chi

Moderation brings harmony and productivity. See Hexagram 11, T'ai

A successful and strong man finds refreshing joy from a younger woman. See Hexagram 17, Sui

Disharmony or Imperfect Marriage or Relationship

Above Yang
(On Top: Male Energy)

Sexual corruption by indulgence of the couple. See Hexagram Ku, 18

A disordered relationship accomplishes nothing. See Hexagram 64, Wei Chi

Divergence between the couple. See Hexagram 12, Pi

A reluctant or arranged marriage. See Hexagram 54, Kuei Mei.

The immortality of nature is in the secret interplay of Kan ☵ and Li ☲, water and fire. Thus, nature is the background of all lives and is the model for the major Kan ☵ and Li ☲. All individual lives are the models of the small Kan ☵ and Li ☲, the interaction of watery and fiery energy. All is nature. Lao Tzu describes the principle of wu wei, which means no extra work is needed in order to attain a natural life, it means life keeps going on without needing interference from the analytic mind. Many practices and small techniques propounded by teachers seem, according to this truth, unimportant, because immortality or longevity is not achieved through doing extra work outside of nature itself. True achievement comes when you enlarge the small foundation formed in your life by the marriage of Kan and Li onto the larger foundation of the marriage of Kan and Li in cosmic nature. Thus, you can realize true happiness by mutual help and mutual completion of the two kinds of energy that in some way conflict with each other. No achieved masters in immortal history were achieved by using the same small practices and techniques, although they can be considered auxiliary measures. Teachers and people generally can utilize such work as internal exercises, for example, all the varieties of chi gong practice. There are numerous ways to help a life to be healthy. All successful practices are aimed at bringing our overly externalized energy back into our natural life beings.

In Taoist achievement, all teachings are used as tools to carry you on to a further stage. Permanent achievement comes from your own gradual development and lighting up. Your power of unobstructable vision is attained when you confirm for yourself the truthful knowledge and practices to achieve yourself. In the long history of spiritual pursuit, a person losing health, energy, a good external condition or life through learning the wrong things is common. In reality, nobody else can determine your choice; it depends on the maturity and stature you have achieved by yourself through your own persistent efforts.

Chapter 7

No Harmony, No Paradise

In the early generations, religious leaders looked for paradise outside in the world. Surely, this was escape. This would not be successful. Even if they found one somewhere, once people moved to such a wonderful place, in no time evil political power or competition would develop and turn into fighting and evil war. A beautiful world would be disturbed or destroyed. Therefore, there is no paradise for human people, unless they learn to get along harmoniously with one another.

Here I offer an outline of millions of years of human evolution. In these next few pages, I wish to call up the image of this time. Then the spiritual seed of a harmonious world may be sown in your fertile spirit and sound mind. A better approach towards a great harmony will be produced if started from you by your attainment of spiritual outgrowth from the muddy world.

I

Knowing Where We Come From, Knowing Where We Go

The learning of Tao is not the partial achievement of mind. The learning of Tao is improving the internal and external reality to bring about complete development. People of the new generation lose themselves in the torrent of drastic new changes. History seems cut short by scholars because the early part of human history is not found in the history books. Yet, if you clearly study it, you can set your own direction in worldly life. Here, I have put together all the bits and pieces of the ancient relics in order to serve those like myself who do not wish to be misled by the limited understanding of history as told by society.

The history I am giving here was removed from the history books by later generations. It seems that each generation likes to establish its own version of history. This happens especially under communism. However, such rewritten histories prevent the new generations from learning important lessons.

II
History is not Always Wise, But it Teaches Wise Students

At its beginning, human society had no establishment of any kind: no government, no family system, no anything. All of those structures arose over time. It is interesting to observe ancient Chinese society and understand the process that molded human society as we know it today.

In China, around 3,000 years ago during the beginning of the Chou dynasty (1122-256 B. C.), we know there were about 500 feudal lords. The number 500 is not accurate, because in a small country there are still many other smaller community leaders. The number 500 was found in the historical records that described the cooperation that abolished the tyrant Jow (reign 1150-1122 B. C). I use this number as a symbolic number, because the number of small kingdoms varied in different times. However, the knowledge that these feudal lords did exist tells us that each community had its own king or leader who could be merely a symbol, a person with not much power or duty, but who was necessary as a focus for the center of the community. A king, prince, duke or feudal lord as a conquering political power was something that arose afterwards when competition began among people.

Thus, at the end of the Sharng Dynasty (1766-1121 B.C.), King Wen united all 500 kings, and together they fought the cruel Emperor Jow.

The Hsia Dynasty (2207-1767 B.C.) ended through revolution and the Sharng Dynasty (1766-1121 B.C.) began. The Sharng Dynasty fell and thus the Chou Dynasty (1121-256 B.C.) began. Both dynasties ended the same way, by revolution. A new central government was established. The revolutions bringing the fall of both of those dynasties both arose for the same reason: because the last emperor of the each dynasty abused his authority and ruled through cruelty. The Chou Dynasty was different. It did not end through revolution, but because the central government had become weak.

As a point of reference, the historical events occurring in Western society at this time were as follows. In 1320

B.C., Moses led the Hebrew people from Egypt and climbed Mt. Sinai to receive the ten commandments. This was the beginning of Judaism. In 1100 B. C., Saul established the Hebrew Kingdom. In 1000 B. C., Zoroaster established his religion. Hindu society also became divided into four classes or castes. In 1000 or 900 B.C., Greece was in the time described by Homer. In 622 or 557 B. C., Sakyamuni Buddha was born. In 551 B.C., Confucius was born. In 521 B. C., King Darius Hystaspis of Persia was enthroned. In 509 B. C., Rome began the system of the republic and began an accurate historical record. In 500 B.C., The Indian Dynasty of Nando was prosperous. In 492 B. C., Persia sent its first expedition to Greece. In 479 B. C., Confucius died. In 477 B. C. Sakyamuni died. In 336 B.C., Alexander the Great was enthroned. In 326 B.C. Alexander the Great invaded India. In 303 A.D., the Romans were brutally persecuting the Christians. In 313 A. D., Emperor Constantine of Rome allowed the establishment of Christianity. In 630 A. D., Mohammed occupied Mecca and became a leader of the Arab world.

These three dynasties, Hsia, Sharng and Chou, set a precedent in Chinese history. Before these three dynasties, each emperor had been elected by the people or chosen by the previous emperor, and was supported by the kings of the small feudal kingdoms. In exchange for support from the kingdoms, the emperor recognized those small kings as independent sovereigns. This custom continued until the Chin Dynasty (248-207 A.D.). We will discuss more about the Chin Dynasty later.

At the beginning, there was no emperor. Then, when the crisis of the big society happened, a common leader of all smaller communities was needed. The emperor was one of the kings who became the leader of all the other lords to successfully respond to whatever special situation was present. Fu Shi (no accurate time was recorded), the developer of herdsmanship, was one such person. Shen Nung (reign: 3218-3078 B.C.) was the developer of agriculture, and the Yellow Emperor, (reign: 2699-2596 B. C.) was the defender of common security and was the cultural leader of the new time. The emperor himself could be someone who suddenly changed from being a commoner or civilian to become an emperor, or he was one of a big number of natural leaders who slowly gained more and more respect from the others. During the crisis, he naturally took the lead and was named emperor. He then gave titles to the natural leaders who were supporters of the central leadership as kings or feudal lords; however, the foundation was still regional.

So a custom then became established. After the emperor or central government recognized the kingship of the small countries (the feudal lords), then the relationship between a central government (emperor) and the satellite states (feudal kingdoms) was established.

But at the beginning, there was no such thing as government at all. An emperor arose above many small kingdoms simply because, as one of the kings, he did a better job. His way of ruling people and his particular tribe or community were so dynamic and influential that he received recognition and support from all the other kings and became the central symbol as emperor. This symbolic emperor did not need to develop or do anything to the entire territory of the 500 kingdoms. His foundation was his small tribe, the small community he came from. He was the symbol of the entire territory, that is all. He needed to render his service and use his personal influence to unite the big nation within the territory of the four seas, as the ancients termed it.

The emperor functioned as the central symbol and held the territory together as the middle kingdom. He did not directly rule people, but he was admired and respected by the other kings. At the beginning, it was not that the emperor was more powerful and won emperorship by conquering the other tribes. Surely it meant that he was the strongest one in his own small community, but it did not mean he had the strength to conquer the other 499 small kingdoms. Being emperor was pure spiritual practice, pure service, pure virtuous extension.

Although this was the first emperor among the 500 kingdoms, the system of having an emperor came much earlier. The proof of this comes from Pang Gu, the Emperor of Heaven, the Emperor of Humans, the Emperor of Earth, the Emperor who brought the use of fire, and the Emperor who taught people to build shelters as dwellings. All of those emperors are from different time periods and represent a certain stage of development of the ancient humans. Each period or time represented by the term "Emperor" may cover a million years or several millions years in the early periods.

Fu Shi was a special individual; he developed the yin-yang system. He was considered a symbol that represented a long period of human development known as the period of herdsmanship. He served as the center of society, and he and several generations of his family enjoyed respect as symbolic rulers of China.

After Fu Shi came Shen Nung (who reigned from 3218-3078 B. C.). He was credited with having begun agriculture. During his time, the political system was in a primitive form; the leader was the symbolic center of ancient society. The system of passing down leadership from one family member to another was confirmed by Shen Nung's family. Their rulership lasted for eight generations, or 520 years. During the development of new agricultural life, the labor force of man was recognized. Because of that, the man-centered society was naturally extended from the earlier mother-centered family system of the ancient people.

The descendants of Shen Nung continued as political heirs until the cannibal tribes, the so-called eighteen Heavenly brothers, started a riot. Chih Yueh was the leader of the eighteen Heavenly brothers who existed in the Chinese region, but had become too strong. They became a great menace to the early cultural life of the big society. By their savagery, they were a destructive force to human progress. Shen Nung's descendants were unable to maintain peace during this disastrous time.

II

The Yellow Emperor was the son of an old leader of the tribe of the star of the Great Bear and had been elected to the military mission to fight Chih Yueh and the eighteen Heavenly brothers. A boy at sixteen or seventeen is at his strongest, and has the toughest energy for battle. The Yellow Emperor was different from ordinary teenagers, who usually only know enjoyment or fighting among themselves over trivialities. I would surely like to see ordinary teenagers guided to use their energy in that more useful direction.

The young man's mission was not simple and he knew that he could not do it alone. He needed support and was perceptive enough to look for wiser people to help him accomplish the big task.

Before the battle with Chih Yueh and the 18 Heavenly brothers, the Yellow Emperor did not have his title. Yellow Emperor was a title he received from his people after he succeeded in restoring peaceful order among all the kingdoms in his area. All of this occurred about 2,000 years before the Chou Dynasty (1122-256 B.C.). There were probably 500 kingdoms, more or less, at that time. He eventually won the battle with Chih Yueh by consulting with some wise people who helped him develop the compass, thus enabling him to locate the enemy in a thick fog.

After he restored peace and order to his people, he was made emperor. After nineteen years of being on the throne, there was nothing for him to do because all places enjoyed great peace. Each community took care of itself, so as emperor, there was no job for him to do unless he wished to establish some kind of interference, but he did not. To cause interference or trouble was not the Yellow Emperor's intention as director of Taoist culture. So he had time to learn herbal medicine, develop clothing, improve the social system and go to the mountains to look for a teacher to study immortal Taoism. He did so many beneficial things for his people that he became considered the father of Chinese culture. But surely, we cannot forget that before him, similar important contributions were made by Fu Shi and Shen Nung.

I believe that at the time of the Yellow Emperor, the emperor and all other men really enjoyed more sexual life. They needed a big population to engage in taking care of cattle and farming the land. That was the first priority of the society. Therefore, men had many wives with the intent of producing many children to work the land and also make the tribal force stronger. I cannot say that the tendency to have many wives is perfect according to the modern view. But at the time of the Yellow Emperor, most men had lots of women. The sages were fortunately wise enough not to kill themselves by too much sex. Moderation in sex is part of their wisdom.

Afterwards, long after the time of the ancient achieved ones, all Chinese emperors had lots of women, but because of too much sex, few lived long. They did not learn that when you face a big feast, you still need to know your limitations and not overeat. The later generation emperors did not have that wisdom. But that is not the point of this discussion. I wish to talk about how slavery developed.

III
Slavery was a Social Fashion

There was no one leader who developed the system of slavery, because as I told you, it was a natural community. Some people had more skills in agriculture, herdsmanship and farming, so other people came to be students or assistants to them. They became followers of those who had better minds or more experience in management of animals and agriculture. Slavery did not develop from people teaching others how to hunt, because any group of people that come together for hunting does not last long. Usually hunting was done in spring or summer, and after all the people shared or divided the meat, everybody would go their separate ways. But for the purpose of raising cattle and tilling the land to have grain, people needed to stay all year.

However, once there was a distinction between the leader or head and the workers, slowly some people came to like living under somebody else's management. It really could not be considered a system of slavery, but eventually it came to be. The natural community changed because some people became dependant and desired the position of subordinates. Thus, the slave system, at the time of its origin, was not only the fault of the leaders, although they should also take responsibility for its creation. It was also partly the fault of the followers, who became overdependent or over authorized the leaders in decision making. This was the key point that brought about the development of slavery.

Afterwards, the followers needed to ask the leaders before doing anything. They would rather give up their freedom and let the leaders manage things: "Okay, you tell me what I am going to do." Then they developed a social custom or a new life style of dependency. They became tightly tied as the followers, workers and ministers to a king. The people said, "We will do whatever you wish us to do, just tell us what it is."

Once somebody died for the king while carrying out an assignment or mission, and was respected or honored by the king and the living followers. Soon this became a social fashion, and people believed that there was glory in dying for the sake of the king. This kind of event became custom. Later, when somebody offered some good advise to the leader or king and the king did not like it, he believed that he had the right to determine that person's life and death. So slowly, things got worse. An undeveloped human could be spoiled by a new establishment, could take advantage of a situation, and could kill people who disobeyed. Originally no contract was made, because there was not any written language. All of this happened during the time that knots were tied in rope as a means of keeping records of events.

So the human mind was spoiled. The power of the kings, queens and lords became spoiled. It was partly due to the undevelopment of the leaders, but it was also the undevelopment of the mass of people who assigned so much authority to the ruler due to a lack of independent spirit.

After the custom of the ruler having the power of life and death over his subjects was established, it became an unwritten agreement in the relationship between the king and his ministers or subjects. That agreement could be verbalized something like this: "You cannot have your own freedom. You must approve of what the king does, says and enjoys. You must do what the king says."

Thus, this all started from social fashion. You see, at the end of the Sharng Dynasty (1766-1121 B.C.), Emperor Jow (1154-1122 B.C.) loved his woman and only took advice from her. Several important capable ministers offered better advice, but he refused it. He thought they were making trouble for him and started to believe they were an obstacle to his authority, so he ordered a cruel way to kill them. Actually, at the time of Jow, the ministers could have refused the death penalty; their option was to leave. However, they did not because it was not considered honorable. It was too late; Chinese society at that time respected the one who would die rather than disobey. At that time, the emperor was considered divine, and so people followed what he said, whether he was right or not. So the ministers were killed.

However, after the ministers were killed, all the bad spiritual qualities of King Jow such as evil, greed and desirousness were fully expressed, and the world understood what kind of person he was. That gave a chance for King Wen to organize and unify the 500 feudal lords. Actually, he only made the strong connection between them and made the preparation for the revolution. It was understood among all of them that the question was, "So now what do we do?" "If we do not do anything, we shall be killed, one by one," was the answer. Looking for survival, he brought them all together to reach an understanding of the situation. King Wen himself did not start a revolution, but he understood it was necessary for Jow to corrupt himself further before they could take action. It was Wen Wang's son, King Wu (reign 1122-1115 B. C.), who started revolutionary military action to depose the emperor after King Wen's death.

IV
Military Strength is the Sovereign

With the defeat of Emperor Jow, King Wu founded the Chou Dynasty (1122-265 B.C.). In it, history turned a new page with great changes. During the first part of the Chou Dynasty, when the capital was in the West, the emperor was a symbol of unity. The emperors of the new Chou Dynasty received recognition and support from the feudal lords. However, the dynasty was corrupted.

During the second part, the capital was moved to the East. The dynasty was reestablished, but the prestige, splendor and glory of the dynasty were falling.

When King Wu, the last emperor of the West Chou dynasty (reign 781-770 B.C.) was in power, he had the same trouble as Emperor Jow of the previous dynasty. He corrupted himself. He did not carry a good image of a spiritual leader. He was the one who ordered the starting of the bonfires for the sole purpose of pleasing his beloved woman and making her smile. The bonfires were used as a signal between the central government and the feudal kingdoms to call out the armies of all the nations to come rescue one another from danger. This means that the emperor used a distress signal to call in the armies of 500 kingdoms only to make his woman smile. Needless to say, that caused trouble for the emperor.

From that event, the spiritual prestige of the emperors declined greatly. During the next part of the Chou dynasty, the capital was moved. The government was reestablished in the East with the help of some feudal kings to try to restore the image of the central government. However, the image of the emperor as the focal point of a benevolent and strong unified leadership was already corrupted and weakened.

Thereafter, things became much worse. The period called Spring and Autumn began with tremendous political turmoil and social disorder. From 722 B. C. up until the Warring Period began (403 B. C.), the chaos increased. In 403 B.C., the emperors in those two periods could no longer hold the nation together as a unified whole; each feudal kingdom wanted its own sovereignty to have the actual control of rulership.

During the Period of Spring and Autumn, five main leaders competed, each one trying to gather his own support and cooperation from the smaller leaders in the area. However, during the Warring Period, almost all of the 500 small kingdoms fought each other. Of all 500, there were seven main or stronger kingdoms that began an intense competition among themselves for control of the entire 500 kingdoms. At last, after many battles, the feudal kingdom of Chin emerged as the strongest military force and therefore became the leader, founding the Chin Dynasty (248-207 B.C.). When Chin's strong military force defeated the other six, the central territory of China again became a unified empire. However, this time it was not by election, but by force.

China was now united under the rule of the first emperor of the Chin dynasty (reign 246-209 B.C.). He was the one who built his tomb and equipped it with an entire army of statues carved out of stone. It consisted of 500 stone soldiers and horses with weapons, armor and chariots. However, the enormous group of artisans who worked to build the tomb were shut alive in the tomb because the tyrant ordered that nobody who entered his tomb should leave it.

During the Warring Period, when a king died, his minister, especially the one who served him most closely, his wives and servants were all buried alive in the tomb with him. The purpose of this was to serve the king in the other world. Is this not cruel? How did this custom start? At the beginning, no such custom existed. At the beginning, somebody loved his leader, loved his king or queen. So when the king or queen died, he killed himself. He died for loyalty, and for the love of his king. Starting from that, a fashion or custom was created that once the king or queen died, the servants must all be buried to go to the shadow world with their ruler.

V
The Restructuring of Society

In human history, few people have expressed wisdom. The majority have only followed their own impulses and desires, or social custom. Impulse and force are still the main kinds of behavior in most situations. Wisdom is a special gift.

In a natural society, only a few people become rich. However, there is no absolute safety for rich people. History has shown us that people of wisdom are not always people of wealth. Although wisdom is different from wealth, it is just as hard to attain. Neither wealth nor wisdom brings good result to its new owner if it is stolen. Wisdom is something that has to be achieved by oneself; it cannot be taken from another person.

In a well ordered society, people of wisdom can enjoy themselves materially and also have high spiritual attainment. This can only happen when wise people are leaders of society. When foolish people are leaders of a society, things are different. When a country's leadership is based on the result of competition for personal aggrandizement, rather than the giving of service to the citizens, wise people retreat from leadership and from being visible. This was the new trend beginning with the first emperor of the Chin Dynasty. It started the necessity for military competition to obtain the throne after each certain period of time of long or short duration. The turmoil and disturbance created by the military change of dynasties each time caused much cultural and social damage and filled the enormous volumes describing twenty-five periods of Chinese history.

Thus, in an earlier stage of history, a change in government would happen after a long time of peace, at least several hundred years. Now bad leaders produced more frequent changes, and more trouble to society.

A tighter structuring of Chinese society began with the advent of the Chin Dynasty (248-207 B.C.). At that time, the need to unify the country under the concentrated central authority of an emperor caused the removal of all the feudal kings. Then each geographical area was divided into counties or provinces, and governors and magistrates were assigned by the central government to oversee them. The central government now had full control of all the small places. No balance between the central government and the local communities existed. By this I mean, there was not an even balance of power between the central government and the local communities as there had been before; now all the power rested with the central government.

Thus, previously the foundation of authority rested with the people or the base of society. Now authority came from the top. The small communities come to be subjects of the central government. Distribution of power can be demonstrated by the image of a pyramid. A pyramid is small on top and large on the bottom. That is the normal distribution of power or authority in a natural society. This means that more power rests with those on the bottom than those on top. However, beginning with the Chin Dynasty, this was reversed so that the bottom of the pyramid was now on top. In the sense of political power, the largest amount of power was in the hands of a few on top, a big government with a big army and many troops. The top held lots of authority, but on the bottom, nobody had any authority. No individual had any political rights. This new establishment changed the fortunes of people in the world.

From then on, the system of monarchy became firmly established with the emperor ruling. Nobody other than the emperor could decide anything. People who wanted power for their own ends, cunning people, knew that there were only two ways to become rich. The ambitious people of the day chose to please the monarch to become rich. The second way was to wage a war, gain territory and wealth and become a rich monarch yourself.

Upright people, people of principle, do not need to do that. They do not like to obtain what they need for their simple lives by bending themselves to please somebody else. They liked to live far away from the political center, somewhere that the ruling force could not reach.

Thus, in those days, the only way for people to become rich or noble was to please the emperor. But those people usually had no high character or high personality. They risked their lives to obtain wealth in this way, because if the emperor was in a bad mood, he could easily behead them.

Chuang Tzu (? - 275 B.C.) lived before the reign of the first emperor of the Chin Dynasty. He had clear vision about what had happened and what was happening, and he wrote a book about it.[1] It was of great value because it spoke in favor of the subtle law and against the existing aggressive warlords. He had to write it partly in metaphor

---

[1]At the request of his students, Master Ni has translated and elucidated this book. It is available under the title, *Attaining Unlimited Life* - editor.

to accomplish the great task of teaching the truth he had received from the Taoists before him. His book was hard to read and accept by the people of his time who were caught up in the social fashion of pleasing the king.

So politics was no longer in the hands of wise leaders or wise people. Politics came to mean dirty dealings, crooked words, false control and bribery. Occasionally, since then, there has been a few comparatively wiser emperors, who would give people a break. But from the Chin Dynasty down, most of them were foolish. Fortunately, the governmental system in ancient times was still very superficial, not very developed or deeply entrenched in people's lives. Sometimes the people needed to give part of their grain to the emperor, or be mobilized for special labor like building the Great Wall or digging a water channel for transportation. Or the people would need to send some men to fight a war for the defense of the border. But because the central government or local government in the city was too far to reach everywhere, people living in the countryside were far away from political influence and still had a good life.

VI
Human Society is the Affair of People

Fortunately, I thank Heaven that during the long period until the end of the Chin Dynasty, even extending beyond it to the thirty-eight years under the Republic of China sponsored by Dr. Sun Yat Sen, Chinese life continued to be the same way. Politics had little direct dealing with most people, especially if they lived in the countryside. Most civilians were free, if they did not choose to become involved in politics. People living in the countryside were not bothered much at all. All people suffered in wartime, whether it was during the invasion of border people, or in modern times during the foreign attempts at colonialism. But people always had a break because they could keep their lives outside the machinery of politics. The real problem of governmental control over people's lives came when communism, a new system of slavery, was imported into China.

Before communism was established in China, nobody openly attacked the ancient ethics of Chinese society. Nobody openly denied the value of morality. Magistrates and governors were primarily chosen to rule counties and provinces through examination or because of their special achievements and merits. Thus, they were mostly good people, but not necessarily wise. A few were cunning, evil people. Moral standards and ancient ethics were respected by people in government and extended to all. People could be evil and secretly make plans to cheat people, but they could not openly become bad people, because society would not accept it. The daughters, sons and family members of someone who defied the moral order would be humiliated and would disown him or her from the family.

Unfortunately, the success of the communist revolution came from denying traditional morality and ethics and ignoring the basic moral nature of people. This created an atmosphere for radical and violent action. Denying people's virtue and moral nature was the worst thing the communists could possibly have done. Why did they do so? Because they wished to gain control of the nation. They accomplished their ends by bad means; they used bad local people. They turned the people into slaves and made communism the boss. That is how they exercise their control, but it is evil ruling.

The previous leaders of society, even if they were placed by the central government, were respected gentlemen or people of prestige, at least on the surface. Now, with the change to communism, although there was better control by the government over many aspects of people's lives, the leaders were people of inferior character and no moral or spiritual education but lots of ambition. They were evil-minded people who disrespected or denied traditional morality and standards of ethics. They were highly recognized by the ruling authority. Those people were put in their positions as tools of the central government to control the nation.

In a normal society, people who are appointed out of special accomplishment have more knowledge, enthusiasm, morality, virtue and dedication to the benefit of the public.

Those people were the ones put in positions of power. Now under the communist rule, those virtuous people became subject to communist persecution and slaughter. Virtuous people are the only ones who have to offer something valuable to the people. They hold office and lead a country in the way of good ideas and moral conviction. Morality is not just an idea; it is a means to make things equitable and fair for all people. In other words, morality makes things function well.

However, those upright people were now called reactionaries or anti-revolutionary criminals by the communists, who believed that such people needed to be killed with no mercy. All people with old moral concepts were suppressed so that the new government could accomplish its purposes. Communism was forcefully promoted as the new religion of slavery for all people.

The new center of the society, the communist party, used destructive means to give bad people power and to compel people to obey the party. Bad or immoral people were told that they could share the political booty. However, to make the situation worse, the communist party itself split into two factions over the issue of executive authority. Destruction increased greatly.

When I was a child, there were only a few bad people in each community. Most people were honest and earned a good living. A few people did not work but instead spent every day gambling or taking opium as their life activity, so each community had a few rascals. Those rascals were greatly valued by the communists who gave them rewards for controlling the community if they spied on others. The communists used underhanded means to attack the people they feared, the ones who might attract people's support by their wish to return to good politics and good social education.

With communist leadership, the quality of politics in China suddenly turned 180 degrees. The new government has used a spy system to control people and take away what people have earned for themselves. Then the communists have centrally controlled the goods and resources of the nation and thus maintained further control over the people.

Ordinary people have no way to disobey them. If people do not listen to them, they will not give them coupons, and then the people cannot buy anything. Once your stomach, your life, is controlled by someone, what can you do? You have to listen.

However, history has proven that whenever people are repressed, a way is eventually found to restore normalcy to society. I hope this will happen in China before long, although it seems that perhaps it will take a little time.

Theoretically, communism strongly cemented the slave system of ancient society. Its control has been so strong and thorough that no people of the nation have escaped slavery. Local governments are controlled by the communist party; the party is controlled by the boss, called the chairman. The boss establishes a typical military dictatorship, a typical evil monarchy system over all people.

The first emperor of Chin was powerful in military and political control. However, his empire and his authority were still stolen by his minister. The emperor's life and his dynasty were cut short because of his cruelty, and after his death, his son was managed by the emperor's evil ministers. Yet the change in government was not caused by an external war or invasion. The enemy of the strong ruling system was inside the emperor's own house. It was his wife and son who were next to the emperor himself, who witnessed the evil and weakness of the emperor and learned from him. This gave an evil minister an opportunity to play his scheme over them and steal authority. This type of internal corruption that occurred during the Chin Dynasty is the same thing that is happening within the communist party today. Society cannot make any advance because of the preexisting internal conflict and defeat within the government itself.

Communism has already died in the minds of the Chinese people. The so-called communist hard-liners hold a tight grasp on Chinese political control, which is backed by the military strength of the army. The real support of the government does not come from people, it comes from the army. It is not a natural society as I described before. The hard-liners are not people who directly engage in producing goods or earning money; they rely on controlling other people. They take people's produce and enjoy the fruit of other people's labor. They still hold on to the communist teaching. They are attached to that conception and scheme to control Chinese society.

Are they acting from the intention to improve people's lives? No, their policies come from their selfishness. Those people can never become rich, because they only work on scheming and bureaucratic paperwork in the office. They are not involved in direct production. They can never make more money.

In China, after the communists seized power, they persecuted four kinds of people: 1) those who had money from inheritance or their own lifetime of hard work, 2) those who were educated 3) those who had social prestige and 4) those who had spiritual faith. I have mentioned only four types of people who were persecuted. There is a fifth. It was political rivals. Most Chinese are traditional people and do not have a sense of politics. But the communists considered all four kinds of people as their political enemies.

Anyway, the force for this persecuting action came from their jealousy. They needed to persecute those they envied. They pushed this practice to extreme cruelty, even extending it within blood relationship to parents, sons and daughters, and among brothers and sisters. The hardliners considered kindness and mercy to be human weakness, a block to the success of communism.

I would like to tell about the knowledge derived from one way the communists persecuted people. Some photos were secretly taken and exhibited in Taipei when I was on the island. They made the persecuted person, the so-called landlord, dig a hole in the ground and get in. The "comrades" then filled the hole, only allowing the head to stick out. The body seemed that it could still breathe because the head was exposed. However, all the internal pressure would build up and come to the head of the person. Then after a certain time, they would make a light hit with a shovel on the head, and the head would suddenly burst, like a small volcano. They did this to many people at the beginning and before they seized the ruling power as an example to tame or subdue the rest of the earnest Chinese people. And by doing this, they became an unquestioned authority. Ever since 1949, the communist party has successfully been in control of the ruling power. During those forty years, the winds carrying the offensive smell of flesh and rain of blood has not stopped for one day.

Communism is established by jealousy. The communist leaders still hold onto that psychology. They do not like to see any other individual, family or China itself achieve and do well through personal effort to become prosperous. They sit in the buildings of the government and allow no one to have a say against the special privileges of the conquerors of people. So no improvement or progress of Chinese society has been seen.

So out of jealousy, those party members hold onto communism as the everlasting truth for all Chinese people. Those people have no openness to allow other people to have money or have a better life. They sit inside the governmental buildings, looking only for what they can enjoy and doing very little real work.

Human society is the affair of people. Only when people change and develop themselves, only when people attain a better understanding, can the world and society be changed. Any external force brings only struggle or suffering, not development. We can see that all evil and suffering is caused by people themselves, by the undeveloped mind. If there is an external force or control, people cannot accept it. There are people who like to impose their ideas upon other people. However, in the political world, all people have the right to choose what is right and who is right to manage the public. The people of self-aggrandizement think they are sages who should be the leaders of modern China. They coax people to listen to them and join them in forcing the majority to obey their idea. Out of good intention or bad intention, before a person really becomes wise, he or she brings about bad things and bad fruit by immaturity. It is evil fruit. This is exemplified by the communist revolutions in Russia and China and the dictators in charge who are promoted to be religious messiahs or saviors. Practically, they do more damage than help to their countries.

During the time of the Warring Period (403-207 B.C.), some people offered to be buried with their dead king or queen. This cannot be judged as good or bad, but it is definitely foolish. In modern China, Mao Tse Tung has already died. The people who followed Mao Tse Tung have a similar psychological attitude like the loyal followers who wished to die with their king. The followers of Mao Tse Tung are still attached to the dead soul of Mao Tse Tung and still keep communism in China.

Why doesn't the Chinese communist party have willingness to loosen its hold to let China go back to freedom? It is because the partisans of the party do not wish other people to achieve better in life by living in a free society. Those people, as I told you, have no traditional moral spirits. There is no traditional or general ethical standard, and they are the ones who tightly hold the reigns of Chinese society.

VII
The Harmonious Way

In my book, *Moonlight in the Dark Night*, there is a chapter entitled, "Clear Choices: Selective or Minimum Involvement." In it, I give the ancient Taoists' attitude toward the world's social environment. Spiritual learning involves all aspects of life. It is important to have a clear understanding of your world so that you know what to do to and where to go to find your spiritual growth. Because life is so precious, we cannot take any chances but must make wise choices.

If you are observant, you will see what you read about the ancients reflected in world events today, and you will know what choices to make for yourself, your good healthy life and your spiritual evolution. You will also come to see a good direction for your service to the world, based upon your skills. "Clear Choices: Selective or Limited Involvement" is an understanding of forces in society today.

Who are the majority of people? We are all part of it, because the reality of the majority is the individual people who comprise it. However, although we are part of something larger than ourselves, we must also retain our individuality. If we totally blend ourselves with the majority, we lose ourselves. Each individual needs time to regulate, adjust, improve and develop himself. With this development and improvement, the better regulation of one's life will come back to serve society. This does not mean you go to the mountains for eight months of the year and you come back to serve society for the summer. It means you directly cultivate yourself on a daily basis in your life in the world. Cultivating yourself helps you keep your individuality so that you can keep your moral focus and do not get caught up in whatever the majority believes. Naturally, you feed back your achievement to society, and your presence means that the strength of morality within yourself does not die.

This direction is not radical. It is gentle. However, it takes time to work. A person has to train himself; for some it takes many years. Just as human beings take time to grow, the purpose of doing cultivation is to allow ourselves to have a chance to grow. We need to grow, to keep our vision clear and to remain flexible so that we do not get caught up in what is larger than ourselves. That is the attitude of old Taoists in a new society.

VIII
The Subtle Truth

It is unwise to search for it outside of yourself.
The farther you go, the farther you miss it.
Search within yourself.
It is where you start.
If you think you are it, you are not.
Just by being with it,
You may meet it!

Chapter 8

Continue Our Growth

I
Harmony is the Cornerstone of the Universe

In the quiet morning,
the sun shines upon the
mountain ridge.
Its light searches deeper
into the valley forest.
Only the clear water in the cold stream responds
with the voice of life,
moving over the green moss
on the relaxed stones.

II
The Evolution of Humanity

My purpose in the last discussion obviously is not teaching ancient Chinese history. Its purpose is to use history to illustrate different stages of human spiritual evolution. Now let us review the spiritual evolution of human society. The leaders of human society are symbols which define the stage of development of the followers. Thus we can understand ourselves by understanding our leaders. Let us start by discussing the first stage of human evolution.

A) Pang Gu. Pang Gu is the universe personified. At its beginning, the universe was an energy egg. Pang Gu represents life conceived as an egg. The ancient Taoists also used Hun Tun to describe the energy egg; it was the stage when the human mind knew nothing. It is the stage of being a baby, of not knowing what is right or good, and not having any personal complicated desire or interest.

So the early stage of human evolution hinted by ancient Taoists was described as Hun Tun and Pang Gu. The Chinese words "Hun Tun" mean water that is murky or turbid before it becomes clear. "Pang" means disc, and "Gu" means antique. "Pang" also means anything in round shape; it means egg. We could say that it is the ancient egg stage. These descriptions do not need to be scientific, because we are describing spiritual evolution during different stages of humankind.

B) Emperor Heaven. After Pang Gu and Hun Tun came the second stage, that of Emperor Heaven. During this stage, no other ruler was established besides the sky. People lived with the sky. The biggest thing that came to them was the sky. They did not even know who their fathers were during that time. For a long time they recognized the sky to be their father, leader, emperor or ruler. The sky changes from cold to hot, shining to dark, and so forth.

The stage of Emperor Heaven occurred during the very ancient time. In that stage, people recognized nothing as the authority, because there was no social establishment. They only recognized the sky above them as the highest. Emperor Heaven was not necessarily a person, but was a personification of the sky.

C) Empress Earth. Then came the period of Empress Earth. During this stage, people had some development and knew enough to stay and live in the place they knew and were used to. The earliest people did not know where to live; they kept moving around like deer. Now they stayed close to where they were born. By staying close to home, they could gather more support from their surroundings. This time was called the stage of Empress Earth.

The people who lived during this time probably had awe for the earth because of their experience of being able to gather nutritious food from the earth, but also they had terrifying experiences of volcanoes and earthquakes and other natural phenomena. Their awe shifted from the sky to the earth. They might have thought their relationship to earth was more direct than their relationship with sky.

D) Emperor Humankind. After a long time came the stage called Emperor Humankind. Now people started to have an understanding that they could be either very supportive or very harmful to one another. This close relationship was much more immediate than that of Heaven or Earth. In the living environment, there were many fierce animals, but they recognized that people were the most capable of doing harm.

Thus, at the beginning, people only recognized the sky. Then they recognized the earth and the surroundings where they lived. Then they came to recognize the importance of people. It is self recognition. They came to the stage where the recognition of people towards the authority of life was completed: sky, earth and self. All three can do good and bad toward their lives. Also, because of the new recognition, they saw that it was their own responsibility to improve their lives.

E) Emperor Housing. With the inspiration of the stage of Emperor Humankind, came the stage of Emperor Housing. After a long period of time, people came to know to shelter themselves. After the experience of roaming around like deer, and living in caves, they came to learn to make shelters for themselves. During this time, a person who made a contribution or new invention which improved people's lives was naturally recognized as a symbolic leader. The term "Emperor" was used as a title of respect.

F) Emperor Fire. Then came the stage of Emperor Fire. It was a splendid development for people to use fire. Fire could sometimes seen in nature, and learning how to use and control it was a great development. How long that period lasted was not recorded.

G) Emperor Herdsmanship or Emperor Fu Shi. (Fu Shi means taming the cattle.) Next came the stage of herdsmanship. Fu Shi, the one who developed the system of the *I Ching* was not only a person. Fu Shi was also one period of time in the development of human life. People respected him and his family, and chose his family to be their leaders. Then there was no competition for leadership among people.

H) Emperor Shen Nung or Emperor Agriculture. After Fu Shi came Shen Nung. His time, when farming techniques were developed, was also a distinct period. That period was not only the length of time of one person's life; it is a period during which Shen Nung's family promoted the new agricultural life. Shen Nung was respected, elected and recognized as emperor. He became a principal character in one stage of human life. His family's influence and position in the center of society lasted for 520 years. They reigned for 8 generations.

I) Yellow Emperor. Then came the Yellow Emperor. He put all the development of the ancients together to form the early stage of Chinese culture, including the use of clothing, herbal medicine, acupuncture, military arts and so forth. This was a great epoch of human history.

Human spiritual evolution was divided into three stages by the ancient spiritually developed ones.

In the first stage, people trusted that the sky was the authority of life that sent either blessing or disaster as reward or punishment to people.

During the second stage, people thought the sky was too far away and its covering was too vast to be able to be directly creating special changes in the lives of particular people. Instead, they believed that trouble or blessing occurred depending upon where a person lived. Thus, they trusted that the earth was the authority of their lives by which blessing and disaster were sent to people.

However, after a long experience of living, they discovered that neither the sky nor the earth were the authority of life. The earth and sky did not seem to hold the intentions of either harming or helping people. So the third stage began, in which people recognized that they themselves were the authority that could bring about either blessings or trouble to themselves. A popular conviction was as follows: "When nature makes trouble, there is still escape. When people themselves make trouble, life becomes really difficult." During this time, the authority of life was recognized to be each individual person, himself or herself.

This was the time that original Taoism was initiated. The ancestors attained the understanding that they themselves were responsible for their good or bad fortune. Much later, this spiritual advancement was not attained by the new generations. They started to make their leaders the authority of life rather than themselves.

At the beginning, emperorship was an honorable job; wise and virtuous people were elected. Later, impostors of virtue fooled people's vision and were also elected. Then real trouble started. The false authority brought a long time of suffering.

The ancient emperors were Taoists until after the Great Yu. Later, most of the emperors or political leaders in Chinese history were "sons of a gun" although they still considered themselves as a son of Heaven like previous conventionally honorable leaders. The later emperors were mostly self indulgent people. The worst thing they did was create the opportunity to let evil ministers and wives or queens conduct their government in an evil way. Therefore, the spiritual evolution of the majority was interrupted. It was not promoted by the leadership of lower intention who only struggled for the power of ruling.

III
Harmony Blesses All Lives

In the early times, the emperor was symbolic as the leader of society. Beginning with Fu Shi, the central society started forming. This was something that happened naturally. No contract was made between leader and followers. The leader was naturally selected because of his good personality, special contribution to people or other attraction. With some attraction, people followed. So the ability to lead depended upon having an attractive personality and special skills. The person must also be a spiritual model. If he was not, the person could not obtain support from people and their willingness to help. Thus, the only way to get support was from giving one's own service to people and creating an attraction. That is how a new leader could be established. Each community had the same type of natural leader. At that time, each community was not one family, but several tribes. The tribal leader was the most intelligent individual in the tribe. This is a kind of natural selection of a leader by people of a small kingdom, which is different than a leader taking power through force. Then all the leaders came together to elect or choose an emperor who would be symbolic of the central government.

The word "Emperor" in Chinese means God. This describes the stage of social evolution in which the emperor was a spiritual image.

IV
The Law of Energy Response

Drastic changes were made by the first emperor Chin (reign 246-209 B.C.) who created new political ruling skills based on the view that human nature is bad. Since then, in Chinese history, evil or cunning people have managed the political situation. There have been some bad ones in each generation whose selfish intention and manipulation has become the source of world disaster. Unfortunately, no law can help stop them, because those people are above the law. They are the ones making and manipulating the laws. Thus, society can not improve.

In ancient times, it only took the evil management or manipulation of a few individuals to establish a system of slavery over the people. A new modern form of slavery is accomplished by the communist society. Its actual result is to make people become slaves. It is the tightest system and is worse than any before. Anyone who has studied history cannot deny that this is one of the most abnormal phenomena of human society.

Tao is the normal track of human social evolution and human spiritual evolution. Anything abnormal cannot last long, although it affects people and causes trouble for a while. Human life will still return to the main track of human social evolution, which can be considered the subtle law of universal life. Any abnormal phenomenon that operates against the spiritual law and against human nature cannot last long. Unfortunately, this kind of evil and foolishness of slavery still strongly influences people in certain regions of the world.

You might wonder how an evil force can become established in the world. It happens the same way that a good force can be established: energy response. Evil people attract evil people. Unfortunately, some people on the verge of going to be good or bad have a tendency towards evil temper or evil nature. Once they participate in that evil group, when they discover their mistake and wish to change their lives to a new pattern of life, it is too late for them. They are already entrapped in that track.

Be careful, my friends. Do you really see what kind of nature your leader has? A leader is made by you, by your support. If you support a leader, and later, that leader uses a radical theory or conception, you shall be the one who suffers from the radical movement. Although at the beginning you think those extreme ideas and actions are fun because you can bring some of your emotional expression together with the leader, you may be making trouble. You can share some benefit from the political movement, but finally you, especially during the later part of your life, or your descendants, will all live under the same subnormal establishment until it is dissolved. So do not make trouble at the beginning. If once you make trouble, it is hard for you to change it. Look at the examples from Russia and China, the communist regions.

V
Stay on the Main Track of Life

Taoist learning does not accept that being either good or bad happens solely from either prenatal reasons or environmental conditions. We trust that the difference in behavior comes from the different stage of spiritual evolution. For example, in one family, with both the prenatal and living environments the same or similar, each individual's spiritual shape can be gradually seen to be different. Differences are also noticed during the stage of growth and continually in all stages of life.

The following is the viewpoint of the Tradition of Tao:

1) Good people and bad people are each based in a different stage that expresses where they are in their spiritual evolution.

2) Because spiritual evolution is always proceeding, being good or bad is also changing. This brings about the possibility for improvement.

3) During the procession of spiritual evolution of all people, good or bad is seen in circumstances. Thus, good or bad is not definite to people. This means that there are people on lower levels of spiritual evolution than others. But the lower levels are not the destination of the people. The built-in direction of spiritual growth is within people. Although it becomes confused sometimes, it always keeps pushing the 'bad' people to move to the correct direction of a good life.

4) In the process of life evolution,

a) the correct path of life is named as the middle route of normalcy. It is neutral and does not involve the conception of good or bad. This means everything is in its own right path, thus, there is no need for any particular description. This is traditionally called Tao or the passing path.

b) Along both sides of the main route,

a) the bypath on the right, is called good.

b) the bypath on the left, is called bad.

c) The divergence from the main path extends as extreme. Either the left or the right bypath is a divergence from the main path; each is an extreme.

d) The by paths have a range of being close or far from the main track of life in the middle. If the bypath is close to the main track of life, it is still in the safety range. If it is far away or on the outer reaches, it is in a zone of jeopardy, and is quite extreme. That is a problem. The extreme of right is to harm oneself with things such as idealistic religious extremes. The extreme of left is to harm oneself with things such as materialistic excess.

5) In the traditional Taoist instruction, the direction of spiritual cultivation is to be very content in the main track of life. Thus, it is to eliminate the conceptual entrapment of good or bad. This is termed "wu wei." It means to do nothing extra in order to be spiritual or good.

6) Traditional Taoist spiritual educational principles work to correct the downfall of one's spiritual quality to move back to normalcy. Thus, it is not agreeable to correct a very left extreme with the safety range of the right bypath; only the main track of life is appropriate.

7) There is no exaltation of the far right as the extreme good to be worshipped in practical life.

VI
To Learn the Subtle Truth

To learn Tao is not like doing meditation.
It takes too long to do sitting meditation on a pillow.
To learn Tao just depends on your own understanding.
You simply learn Tao by dropping all irrelevant struggle;
it does not require extra hard work.

To learn Tao is not like religious learning.
There is no value in putting a head
over the head you already have.
You just need to jump out of your psychological traps.
By so jumping, you can directly reach the sky.

To learn Tao is not like intellectual study.
It is complete in itself.
It can be displayed by green grasses growing in the pond.
The simple reality shocks the universe.

VII
Let us Build a World of Great Harmony

As descendants of all the ancient people, we have the opportunity to review the cultural creation of the ancient wise ones. The world is not a peaceful, happy world in some times of history and in some regions. The ancient wise ones, with their special vision, put their effort in a special direction; they wished to work for a better world.

For example, Jesus' idea of the kingdom of Heaven, practically, was his wish to have a world of justice. Has the world become just by Christian teaching? Surely we have not reached there yet. Buddhism offers the pure land. The pure land means basically a world of no war, a world of peace. Has that been achieved? Not yet. Did not both Jesus and Buddha have an excessive focus on the spiritual and rather than working towards improving the world? Or perhaps they did try to help the world through giving teachings, but they were simply not successful. Perhaps they were successful but their followers failed. They were more interested in guiding us to go somewhere else where there is justice and peace.

What does conventional Taoism teach in general? It divides the expansion of human life into two spheres: the pre-Heaven sphere and post-Heaven sphere. Practically, the pre-Heaven sphere is the pure spiritual realm of each individual and of the universe. There is peace, justice and equality in that part of life. The other sphere, called post-Heaven, is the world of physical, separated existence. It is a mess. The Taoist teaching seemed to encourage people to withdraw from the messy world or post-Heaven stage to enjoy the pre-Heaven stage of spiritual or eternal life. However, choosing one or the other is an extreme way to live. Our lives can be balanced to let the post-Heaven serve the pre-Heaven, or let the pre-Heaven guide the life of the post-Heaven. Some Taoists do not do that. They do not face trouble; they go away.

Mohammed offered a different teaching. Mohammed offered the notion of one god. In reality, there is one spiritual law in the universe, but many gods. So there is competition and there is war. In the human cultural level, when one god was established, there was the building of the strength of rejection and denial of other worship. So no peace was brought about.

Mohammed was inspired by Moses' religious creation. Because he was a leader of a small caravan, Mohammed went to China. Being the leader of a caravan simply meant that a person had access to traveling. In China, Mohammed was inspired by the general Chinese people who worshipped the sky or Heaven personified as the Lord of Great Transformation, or the Upper Emperor. Also in China, he observed the way that the monarch around the period of Sui (589-618 A.D.) and the early Tang Dynasty controlled society with cruel punishments and how the monarch exacted obeisance from people by making them kneel down to bow, putting their forehead to the ground. In Chinese, that type of bow is specifically called the kowtow. Those means were used to command people's obedience. This social system did not express any relationship to spiritual achievement. It was a ruling skill, a way of taming the barbaric nature of people by systematic control. This was all adopted by the young Mohammed.

At the time Mohammed visited China, he might have been stimulated by the ruler of that time, Emperor Yang (reign 605-616 A.D.), one of the most debauched and vain rulers in ancient China. Compared to his condition of luxury, Louis XIV of France was a very small example. Emperor Yang had so many beautiful women he gathered from all over the vast country of China. At the same time, he extended cruel control over society by requiring severe punishments. The position of emperor in China was made to be a god.

Mohammed's religious background used Moses' work. Moses' religious framework was based upon Babylonian and Egyptian influence and experience. He insisted upon one God. Mohammed, however, did not declare he was god. He did better than Jesus. Jesus declared himself as God; it aroused jealousy and disbelief among people, although to him, it was the effect of spiritual assimilation.

Thus, the success of the early Tang Dynasty (630 A.D.) gave inspiration to the young Mohammed. It gave him ideas of military adventure. So he took the three elements of control, i.e., religious worship, bowing which expressed absolute obedience and cruel punishment from the old corrupt China with the conventional religion and dominating thoughts of one god. Then, he went home to start a totally new social fashion in that region. When he took Mecca, in the year 630 A. D, he laid down the foundation for the future development of new social customs.

When Moses gave the ten commandments in Sinai in the year 1320 B. C., all those teachings did not come from Heaven. They were all human creation. That is the development of that the good taught the good and the bad taught the bad. If the young Mohammed studied Lao Tzu's *Tao Teh Ching*, his contribution had to be different.

We do see that a society needs to be correctly and wisely guided. A good society offers a foundation for people to learn to live their own lives, look for their own higher spiritual development and give help to society. A good society does not teach people to live a life that someone else organized for the majority over 1,000 years ago. If that were the case, human descendants could never do better than their ancestors. Such a system is backward and does not make progress. Unfortunately, few people study spiritual reality and even fewer attain actual spiritual achievement. Therefore, they are managed by existing tailored styles of behavior. There is also shortcoming of the spiritually developed ones: they do not have a high interest in moving away from their own personal spiritual goal to work to improve the underdeveloped customs.

We may observe the past 3,000 years and conclude that all the wise ones wished to bring something to help the world, but the result of their teachings was only to foster more prejudice and separation in ordinary people. They did not bring about a really good world for people.

My foundation comes from an open teaching. My goal is not to teach the old fashioned notion about the kingdom of Heaven, because the kingdom of Heaven still has a king to make all others as subjects. My teaching is to teach a world of great harmony with equality and justice. This is my goal. All my work and effort during the past many decades contains the wish to develop my friends to have a vision equal to that of the ancient wise ones. Everybody should avoid personal establishment, but offer something to the world. This is where we live.

I talk about a world of great harmony with equality and justice. It is not like the ancient type of promotion in which we need to establish an external deity or an image of a forceful god. When people continue to think that God is outside them, they establish a conflict between what is external and what is internal. God is both external and internal. God is the universe and God is you. Each individual human person is a small model of the world, thus each individual is a world, whether the internal world or the other one needs development.

People who do not understand the value of a balanced life use the mind to command the body or use the body to command the mind. In other words, the desires of the body and the desires of the mind sometimes conflict with each other. That brings difficulty, trouble or tension to a person. The entirety of one's life being becomes distressed. So you need to achieve yourself internally. This means to harmonize all parts of your being so that you can move forward.

An individual who becomes a world of harmony, a world of equality or a world of justice does not use the left brain to command the right brain or the right brain to command the left brain. Because each different body (physical, mental, emotional, etheric and cosmic) has a different function, it extends different desires too. So some people tend to be more physical, while others are more spiritual. That is all a one-sided projection.

We need to achieve a world of harmony, a world of equality, a world of justice. Then we will bring about a really good life for everybody. It is not that in the next life I will become a Buddha, or after ten lifetimes. Instead, I need to change the world to become a Buddha world, become a God world.

I give classes and write books discussing many aspects of life just to give you one message. It is to tell you about the direction we need to go in, and the kind of being we need to be for the maximum health of ourselves and the world.

Each person needs internally and externally to become a world of harmony, equality and justice.

If you look at the past, you will see that the religious leaders brought many ideas to the world. Their intention is beautiful. However, their teachings were limited by the times in which they lived; now we must reevaluate the teachings with regards to modern life. I use my experience of both the traditional lifestyle of pre-communist China and my experience in modern Los Angeles to create a bridge of understanding between the ancient and the modern. We cannot wait for any messiah to come to the world before we find out what and how we can contribute to the world. Each individual needs to be one's own messiah. Each person needs to be one's own savior of the world and of oneself.

This is my main theme. I recommend many serviceable practices of cultivation with the purpose of building good individuals who will work towards a world of harmony, equality and justice. If you understand this key point, then you understand the kind of service I wish to render. I do not wish to be a leader. I am not a leader but a supporter. I wish to offer the advice of the ancients to all people so that they can be the leaders and the supporters. If their conditions are right, young people can establish spiritual centers to help work towards the same purpose. Anyone who has a similar vision and wishes to achieve a world of harmony, equality and justice can do the same, where appropriate.

I have already discussed all aspects of natural healthy life. It may not be enough. However, a harmonious world is the direction towards which we can work together. There is no one individual who in one lifetime or ten lifetimes will be enough to work out the goal of realizing a world of great harmony. If everybody joined one another to work out the goal of attaining the world of great harmony, I tell you this, the job could be done. We can reach there with no problem. I wish with all my spiritual, physical and mental strength that this is where we are going to go.

In ancient times, people would cultivate or discipline themselves alone to bring about the birth of their spiritual fruit. Some people would choose a broad way of spiritual practice and go to the world and teach or promote goodwill and kindness towards all people. Buddhism divides their practices into two types. One is called Hinayana, i.e., the small vehicle and the other is called Mahayana, i.e., the big vehicle. The spirit of each is different. Only a few people can be carried in the small vehicle; the big vehicle can carry many people. They are two different spirits. One spirit, the spirit of the small vehicle, says "Let me stay in the mountain to abandon the world." This established hermits. The other spirit, the spirit of the big vehicle, says "Let me go to help the world." This established religion.

Most religions have followers who go to cultivate themselves in caves or rural places. But they have other followers who go to the world and try to change people's spirits. We need to correct both; we are looking for a balanced life. Stay in the world and work to help people, but also practice personal self cultivation every day. Thus, at the same time, the fruit of your cultivation, a harmonious spirit, is not only enjoyed by yourself, but the world can also share it. There is no selfish God, there is no selfish Buddha.

Worldly or political leaders, those who do not recognize the importance of one's own spiritual position, will turn to be selfish for self protection. Two modern examples are the later leaders of China and Russia who lack spiritual virtue but yield to external pressure for one's own political benefit. They certainly sacrifice righteousness for political survival. This will invite personal humiliation and disaster to the society when it moves towards democracy.

The past religious approach is similar to the physical or military adventure of some Chinese people. They have one term to describe their life policy. "If I am successful, I will be king. If I fail in the military adventure, I will become a bandit." These people were looking for competition in the world's arena. Unfortunately, religious effort was not much better than the competition in the world's political arena. In any field, the lower characteristics or performance of life need to be avoided. Let us all put our personal emotion, personal background, race, religious custom and whatever else we have grown up with into a different category, but let our spirits join together to build a world of equality and justice, a world of Great Harmony.

Chapter 9

The Direction of Human Spiritual Evolution

I
The Subtle Truth

You say that music comes from the instrument.
Why does it not give music when it is kept in the box?
You say the music is in your fingers.
Why do you not just listen to your fingers?

II
Is Human Nature Predecided?

In ancient times, Hsun Tzu (313-221 B. C.) was the student of Menfucius. Before Hsun Tzu and Menfucius, no one questioned whether human nature was good or bad.

Menfucius viewed human nature as good. He said that humans become bad due to environmental influences. Menfucius used the following argument to prove his point: In ancient times, people obtained their water from wells. Most of the deep wells had no railing or protection. If a mother was busy or distracted, and her baby was crawling around the top of an unprotected well, any adult would see the potential danger and stretch out his hand to pull the baby away from the edge.

Hsun Tzu was also quite a respected scholar, but his development and his understanding was different. He observed that human nature is bad. He said that if laws, guidance or discipline were not set up for people, they would do anything they liked, even if it were harmful to others. He claimed that education is required to form a good personality or character and that society especially needs law. During his time, there were no written laws; people did as they pleased. Hsun Tzu said that since regulations, rules or lines are required to bring order to people, human nature is originally bad. If people are indeed good, then why does crime happen? It needs no proof. When someone leaves his home to go to a city or a town, will his luggage be safe if he does not watch it?

So now let us discuss the original nature of human beings and whether it is good or bad. Who was right, Menfucius or Hsun Tzu? Let us go deeper than what they discussed.

Common thought is that either human nature is predetermined, or it is molded by the environment in which a person lives. First, is human nature pre-determined or it is decided by the environment? If human nature is pre-determined, we are all born good. If we are all born good, then why are there so many bad things happening in the world? If you do not guard yourself on a trip, even if you are a careful person, you may lose something. If you are walking on the street and you forget and leave your wallet on a bench where you stopped to rest a while, what chance is there that you will return and find it intact? It seems unlikely, given the crime rate of today, that anyone can believe that human nature is pre-determined as good.

So we have postulated the theory that human nature is predetermined as good. However, if human nature were unquestionably good, then why would so many bad things happen in the world? Even when people guard themselves and their possessions with proper care, bad things still happen. All people know that whether you are out traveling or you stay at home, you must always be watchful. If you are not watchful, someone might take advantage of you. This is perhaps one proof that human nature is not predetermined as good.

III
Environment Is a Factor

The second thought is that humans become good or bad depending upon their environment. This means that the original nature of human people is neither good nor bad; the environment determines the goodness or badness of a person. Thus, each person has the potential to be either good or bad, and the person's expression is variable depending upon the circumstance.

Let us look at an example and see whether the environment does in fact determine a person's expression of good or bad. There are two starving men in the same locale. They see a container in which some delicious refreshment is kept. They could just go over to the container and eat the food without further thought about who owns it, or anything else. That might be the environmental view, that because food is in the environment, they eat. Another approach is that one goes over to ask or beg for the food. A third possibility is that one goes over and makes an exchange to obtain the food. If he does not have the money, he may promise to pay later or work for the food. However, he may hold back from taking anything without paying someone for it.

More specifically, there are two men who have not eaten all day and are very hungry. They go out to the street and see a vendor selling some delicious warm Chinese sandwiches called bao-tse. What will happen? There are several possibilities. First, they may go over and steal the sandwiches. Second, they may go over and ask the vendor to give them some bao-tse, which is begging. Third, they may go over and make an exchange, which means giving either money or work in trade for the food.

Whatever the outcome, it is the same environment. The men's reaction to their own need or personal temptation has various possibilities. In this instance, it is not the immediate environment which determines the men's response. The approach is still determined by each individual's previous environmental conditioning, such as education.

Someone may argue that this example deals with two adult men, and adults come from different environments, backgrounds and education. So maybe it is not the immediate environment that determines the men's approach to obtaining food, but it is the environment of their childhood background. If children are hungry and see food, they immediately begin to eat without even thinking about payment, because they have not been educated. So, the second theory still holds that the environment determines the goodness or badness of a person.

If you study a little more or you understand more about life, you may learn that although environments can indeed superficially affect people's behavior of good or bad, people can also change environments if they want to change themselves. Thus, if the environment is not predetermined and can be changed, then a good environment and good education can help someone become a better person. It is also true that if some people are put in good environments and given a good education, no change will occur.

Certainly there will be a difference between a child who grows up in a normal family and a child who grows up in a den of thieves. But even among two children who grow in the same den of thieves, different tendencies of personality can still be seen. One child may be more cruel or greedy than the other. Why is there a difference? The difference is personal nature. This nature is prenatal nature. In other words, it existed before the person was born.

We cannot deny that prenatal nature is important. One's personality starts forming in the womb of its mother. Each mother is already a teacher to her future baby. The other important factors in determining an individual's personality are the family background or how the mother runs the family, the natural environment of the family and the social environment. For a gentle and sensitive person, education will be a good tool to guide a person to live an upright life. In his life, he will not have anything to do with policemen or criminal courts, unless the person becomes involved with complications of a chain reaction set by somebody else.

A big society cannot give up its police, criminal law and court system, because there are two levels of people. Not all people are gentle and learn from education. If it was a definite fact that all people were bad, then there would never be enough police or soldiers to keep the peace. In that case, even policeman and the army it self would be full of bad people. Then how could the army and the police be controlled?

There are a few people who do bad, making bad choices when they face temptation or a bad situation. Those individuals are not the majority. Most people do not need police or the army to enforce their good behavior. Therefore, most people are normal people and have a normal birth.

IV
Universal Order is Tao

In a normal society, there is no need for classification of whether people are good or bad. It is not necessary to make an argument for whether human nature is good or bad. In a normal society, only a few people are criminals or have behavior so bad that policemen or armies are necessary to guard society from their potentially irresponsible behaviors. Sometimes a government relies on policemen or an army to control people or uses a group of gangsters to rule people in society. Usually it is only when a government is bad that the police or army are called out to maintain control. Unfortunately, there are many leaders in the world today who establish their rulership in this way. Those people are bad and have a deep evil nature. The wise Chuang Tzu said: "One man steals something small and is called a thief. Another man steals a state and is called an emperor." In history, not all governments were good governments and not all rulers were good people. They use an army and policemen to protect what they have stolen and receive obeisance from the less powerful people of the society.

When people use force to obtain political power, society is abnormal. The new rulers have fear in their minds. Because they obtained power by force, they must use force to maintain their power. They know that others would like to follow their example to gain power with force, so they try to strengthen their control by use of secret police or an army. In this way, they control the majority.

Tao is respected as the universal orderly spirit. The universal order designates that nobody extends self-aggrandizement to establish their thoughts or system and impose it upon other people. Why should a government have the right to impose what it wishes upon other people?

In ancient times, when a government maintained its power through violent or physical coercion, it must have felt that its power was in danger. The leaders felt insecure and needed to have more policemen and a bigger army to grasp people more tightly. This type of control expresses human sickness.

V
Improvement is Made By Self-Spiritual Development

Let us go back to Menfucius, who said that human nature is good, and Hsun Tzu, who said that human nature is bad. Hsun Tzu was a respected teacher. One of his students, Harn Fei Tzu (? - 234 A.D.) further developed the theory of Hsun Tzu and wrote a book based on his understanding of how to control people. In other words, he wrote about how to be a monarch of great power using military means. Unfortunately, this book was seen by the young prince of Chin. He adopted the theory that people are bad, and believed that through establishing the fear of threat, people could be controlled like cattle and obey the orders of the monarch. It was effective ruling policy in that time and established a powerful government. Later, it became common practice among governments and is used even today.

So the book of Harn Fei Tzu guided the young prince to achieve his personal selfish purpose to establish the first unified government under one person's control. That was the first emperor of Chin (reign 246-207 B.C.). His reign ended swiftly. Because it did not follow the normalcy of human nature, his regime fell to competitors within his government who did to him exactly what he had done to others. Over and over again in history we see leaders with a similar sick psychology who try the same thing. It always turns out to be disastrous for society.

Even though political leaders and social workers play dirty, if they are of a moral nature, they will improve the world. Religions, although they profess to be morally natured, have hardly made any great contribution to the world during the last 3,000 years. In certain areas they did, such as establishing charitable works, but on the other hand, they have been the cause of a great many holy wars. The developers of religions presented a power competition in a different way. They also could be pushed by bad politics. They were living in darkness. They did not give the most clear spiritual response to the bad social system. We can see that by viewing today's religions. Instead, some religions were established with the same purpose as bad politics, which is to gain social power.

If you limit yourself to religious learning and their teachings, it does not serve a practical function in spiritual improvement. Religion helps more on the level of social control by establishing emotional or psychological programs. The real progress that has been made up to now in some societies comes directly from people's own awakening in politics and social systems. World improvement has been made in some societies. Socially, religion has become less a ruling tool, but serves as emotional support with unclear spiritual vision.

If we consider that Chinese culture started with the Yellow Emperor, it has existed for 5,000 years. During that time, it seems that people have not made any progress in improving human nature, personality or character. It only seems that their nature has become intensified by living in a world with more competition and abnormal experiences. This seems to create fear in people, and makes them wish to control others to achieve an immature goal. Those immature goals are impractical.

You can see that the reality of the world is that there are people of good nature and people of bad nature. Good or bad nature are decided both by environmental influences and prenatal conditions. Definitely, people's nature can find improvement from education to some extent. Mostly, improvement is made by self spiritual development.

People of good nature are more or less disturbed by people of bad nature. In some societies, good natured people are ruled by a small group of bad natured people. The old religious path suggests that the good people surrender, and be submissive or obedient. And the good people do so because they are already nice and do not wish to interfere with other people's business. People who interfere with other people's lives and business are evil. Evil, interfering people are found not only in politics but in religion, too.

The good are controlled by bad in only some parts of the world. This can be corrected if the good people stand up and work things out. They do not need to follow old religious fashion and take persecution when bad people try to oppress them. If you do not make an effort or contribute to the world, the world will hardly be improved. Only when a good system is brought about, and good policy is formalized and made concrete, can it become a strength to restrain bad or evil nature. This is what I see as the only possibility.

In social evolution, politics is the central focus or most influential factor in human life. The general condition of society prepares the foundation of political improvement. The general condition of society is defined by people's intelligence and their means of earning a living. The general condition of society has changed greatly in the last 200 years, starting with the industrial revolution and the application of mass production to all areas of human life. In particular, the rapid development of technology has changed the world. Before that, some historical events happened which paved the way for world progress. The renaissance in western society brought people back to humanity and fostered the idea of democracy.

In ancient times, all societies were viewed as parts of an integral whole society. The evolution of the big society was called Tao. Sometimes it got off the normal track; that is called going against Tao. The term is simple and easily understood.

VI
Circumstantial Behavior is Not True Nature

At the end of the Chou dynasty, during the Warring Period, (starting in 403 B.C.), the spiritual quality of China's leaders changed drastically. Before that period, the foundation of society was the local community. The emperor was just a symbolic center of all the small kingdoms. Unless there was a special reason, the empire was peaceful. Beginning with the period of Spring and Autumn (starting from 722 B.C.), things changed. The princes and feudal lords became more ambitious, greedy and aggressive. Smaller communities were absorbed or swallowed by larger ones. The feudal kings competed for leadership as emperor of the central government.

The feudal kingdom of Chin succeeded over all the others by the strength of its army. After it defeated the other six strong kingdoms, the Chin Dynasty unified China by changing the feudal system into a system of counties and provinces under the control of one man, the emperor. A strong government which ruled over all people was established. This new type of government interfered more in people's lives and demanded more from them. This was out of the ambition of self-aggrandizement. It was not out of the purpose of serving the people.

Menfucius' view was that human nature is good. It is more or less an idealistic vision. It was not the view of the ancient Taoists. They thought that human nature is the same as universal nature; it is expressed as changeable in different situations that can be judged by people as good or bad. Universal nature and human nature mostly express themselves positively. Human nature mostly maintains its normalcy and mostly people live healthy lives. This is good. However, where human nature is overly controlled or circumstances are abnormal or unnatural, humans can be bad.

As students of Tao, we know that circumstantial behavior is not the expression of pure nature. Behavior is mixed with personal energy, mood, disposition, temperament and intelligence. Let us say a child does something that is not agreeable to the parents at two different times. Each time the parent will react differently, because the father or mother is in a different phase of his or her energy cycle. For example, in the early morning, people's minds are much clearer than they are later in the day. In the afternoon, people's energy slows down, and they easily become nervous, tense or irritable. So they will react differently at different times. A certain thing can be pre-judged as good, but because behavior is issued forth from a person's internal energy, and that energy changes, the response will change according to circumstance.

What we think about ourselves always influences us very much. Lao Tzu's first student, Wen Tzu, talked about the need for laws among kingdoms and individuals to be obeyed by everyone. He said that judging people according to fairly applied law is the same as the universe itself which is governed by the subtle law. Wen Tzu presented that concept. Harn Fei Tzu combined it with his teacher Hsun Tzu's view that human nature is bad. He suggested education as the solution to improve human nature. When Hsun Tzu's view of bad human nature came to Harn Fei Tzu, according to Wen Tzu's vision that laws were needed, Harn Fei Tzu concluded that people needed to be managed rather than left to their own instincts. Here, he meant all people, not just bad people. He then developed techniques for how to manage people. One way is for a monarch to determine and apply reward and punishment. Another way is to attract or bait people with positions over others, and make them help the monarch govern other people. In the position of a monarch, you do not need to give people anything, you take things from people and conduct the government. All people were made to accept that as the law.

In Wen Tzu's view, law should not be decided by somebody on the top. Law should come forth by people, from people and for people. It is just like the modern view. Law should be like a contract, upon which all sides agree. Everybody agrees that it is good for themselves. No special privilege is established for anyone and no one can take advantage of others. That is how modern law is made.

But the young Harn Fei Tzu took the Taoist thought of an unified, equal law for all and turned it into a new theory that people need to be managed or controlled, or else they will not obey the monarch. Then, with the purpose of making people obey him, the monarch set up rules to apply to everyone except himself. After he adopted this idea and governed people by the rules and laws he made, the small kingdom of Chin became stronger than any other kingdom.

Before becoming the first emperor of the unified China, the young prince admired the writings of Harn Fei Tzu. Harn Fei Tzu was invited to Chin, but the young prince of Chin discovered that the young man was too smart and so he was jailed and killed.

It is not wise to teach people to become evil. Whoever does will find that all the evil will come back to oneself. The bright side of human nature is the only thing that should be exalted by religion, education and politics.

The politics of Chin were evil. They took the teaching that exalted or acknowledged the dark side of human nature and stimulated a change in people's spiritual quality which has continued since that time. His actions caused people to observe that being bad made a kingdom strong, or being strong made a kingdom bad.

In China, people are still under governmental control today. The laws support the government, not the people. The situation has not turned around yet; the government is still in the stage of downfall.

VII
Undo the Extra Cultural Contamination

In ancient times, when human capability was small, the amount of trouble or damage that a bad person could make was also small. Today, with the advent of modern technology, the amount of trouble that someone can make is much greater. Therefore, even a small boy can make so much trouble that it may take many people to handle it. In ancient times when conditions were natural, even if human nature extended itself in a bad direction, no great harm could be caused.

During these last 3,000 years, focusing on whether people have a good nature or a bad nature is skimming over the surface of reality. In different societies, people have their own customary values of life. In some spiritual or religious traditions, a peaceful person is honored. This is not true of some other communities which offer a war-like personality. These religious customs or social values bring complication to the topic of human nature. Surely it is unnatural development when people of different racial or religious backgrounds, and even different small sects of the same religion, express hostility towards differences. This is the worst kind of spiritual pollution. It is more fundamental than any cultural pollution in covering over the natural, pure mind.

This trend of human development to dislike differences was foreseen by the ancient Taoists. With foreknowledge of this as the cause of future political trouble, the ancient Taoists gave their teaching. They suggested that to restore natural health, a person needs to wash away any cultural dye or coloring that has been absorbed into one's personality. That will also restore the original mind and spirit. Anything else that was learned from the subnormal development of society must be a downfall or burden to the original healthy spirits of a person.

Today, my teaching is no different than that of the ancients. The lessons come from becoming free of the cultural environment. In modern times, this is much more complex than in ancient times. If a person who has sincerity wishes to achieve oneself, the basic thing he must work on is undoing the extra learning which is really unnecessary to the original healthy life nature of a human being. When a person has dropped what is unessential to life, the standpoint of nationality or religion becomes secondary. People's ideas of becoming a hero or an enemy also seem foolish. A peaceful living environment and a peaceful society are the foundation of the health of all individuals and society. This has been hidden from the vision of the leaders who promoted ideas and established teachings.

VIII
The Common Good of All Mankind

When I was small, my parents guided me according to my own nature to learn what general history has forgotten, such as how people developed from stage to stage and whether human nature is good or bad. These questions were like a spark that was kindled inside of me. Through years of accumulating knowledge, I came to know that most human behavior comes from the cultural layers of society. Different societies had different ideas; these ideas shape people's behaviors into certain patterns. Once people fasten onto those ideas and patterns of behavior, differences between cultures are seen. Unfortunately, these behaviors become like concrete and then clash with other people's patterns. This study led me to have a vision of the necessity of restoring one's original human nature before any conceptual differences were developed. The purpose is to reach a harmonious world, paradise or Heavenly kingdom - whatever the ancient spiritual leaders called it.

The establishment of customs or ideas can become stone walls that separate people from one another. Things like a person's religion, nationality, and racial background can become a personal conceptual identification which can create disharmony with other people.

When I was young, I had the idea that I would like to extend my learning to all people, and to promote a world of great harmony with equality and justice by starting a spiritual group called something like, "People Joining for the Common Good of All Humankind." I wished that people would say, "It does not matter what your background is, let all of us be friends." If we continue to hold onto the creations of the past, they will become the obstacles to harmonious life in the world and to the harmonious cooperation of human future. That was in my mind.

I expressed my interest, my goal, my vision to some of my young friends and received their support. We must all come back to face the realistic problems of the world and not stay with childhood idealism. I wished that my work could provide a way for many people to come together. And I wished that my work could help many people on other levels, too.

By studying history, we learn that in ancient times, the more worldly and ambitious people, who were not necessarily wise, grouped together to become a social force. The wise ones always retreated to the rural places or the mountains and had nothing to do with central society. Or they made religion as their protection to escape the political disturbance of their day. This is actually how Zen Buddhism established itself.

Now in this stage of human development, you do not have any way to escape social or political involvement. You also do not like to use religious coloration to cover your true spiritual being. Unwise people grow up to become a force to make the world turn in their direction. Perhaps you are one of the victims of the unwise promotion. This brings the downfall of human spiritual quality.

As Taoists, we do not consider that we are wise; we consider ourselves as students of wisdom. This wisdom guides people to look for the complete development of life that has perpetual value, not something of short momentary good, which is what people are fighting for. So we do not compete for the things that are short lived, such as social glory, etc. Other people are highly interested in such things, but we see that it is not most important in life.

We enjoy a peaceful life of progress with the positive support of the normalcy of our social and natural environments. A student of wisdom needs to find friends who have a similar standpoint in modern society. We would rather be defensive of the good spiritual quality that we are aware of, and appreciate the good quality of life. But we are only defensive, not offensive. Thus, we can also keep open to learning what is new and good, what is improvement and what is achievement.

We have witnessed some religious groups of people. They are defensive, and guard themselves from the downward influences of outside society. By so doing, they also limit themselves and are not open enough to receive new spiritual inspiration, or to flow with the good trend of human progress. New ideas and inspiration give us some knowledge as to how we can practically organize ourselves in our lives.

We feel unhappy about offensive religions and aggressive political principles. These things push humans in the direction of someone's immature wish. That is evil and undevelopment. We cannot stop them, just as we cannot stop our patients from continuing their bad life habits that cause their trouble.

Extreme political movements and offensive religious promotions will cause disaster for human society. They will become an evil force that stops the forward steps of human society.

The quality of modern life has changed from the ancient one's lives. In ancient times, if a person was good and had been good, that person would be left alone undisturbed. Now, in modern times, nobody can live completely alone anymore. You have to belong to some group, and have a clear spiritual or cultural position to tell people that you do not wish to have any offensive religious promoters come to your door. You have to put a sign out that prohibits salesmen from coming to your door.

This new defensive but open spiritual society welcomes people who enjoy peace, and may have a religious or spiritual background with a moderate approach. The group I called Joining for the Common Good of All Humankind would function to express our attitudes in political and social matters. It can be only a spiritual connection or some strong and virtuous leaders who help, if it is done naturally and correctly. Particularly, I would like to emphasize defensiveness with open attitudes towards social progress. We would not cause manipulation for the people in the group, but give service. If there is any financial responsibility, it would be a fair charge.

In a modern society, we face so many commercial, political, social and religious promotions. We need to understand from what to guard ourselves, and to what we can open ourselves. Nobody really knows unless they experience mistakes or trouble for themselves. No one teacher can offer a service for all categories of your life. No parents or elders can protect the young generation from unhealthy cultural teaching of the new society.

I wish this group to do a service for its own members, to be selective and only accept good merchandise. All good and bad experiences can be communicated within the group. Such communication can permit one person's costly experience to be useful to other members such as sexual trouble, unhealthy sexual practices, or bad life experiences. All can become a good reflection for the growth of all the members.

This group should not become directly involved in politics. I would like it to give a good influence to politics and the social direction of society over the long run. The purpose of the group should not be power searching. Nor should there be struggling for anything else within or without this group. They should not wish to extend grouping expansion like the way of other offensive religions. Let the group receive natural growth with different leaders in different regions, and have communication and connection with other centers or groups in different regions. They can work together for the benefit of the society.

Teaching Taoism to you is only secondary or tertiary in my personal intentions. My greatest interest is to have a world of great harmony. The great harmony can only be achieved when justice, equality, responsibility, honor and all good virtues exist at the same time. This kind of good world can start from you and your surroundings. This idea I recommend to all my friends. I wish new spiritual communities can be established in this manner. They can grow naturally with a clear spiritual mission and healthy requirements as a gathering place for all people of self-improvement and non-competition. Such a community should grow organically according to the development of the group. In this way, it is possible for people to come together, benefitting all with reflection, growth and improvement. This can serve as a model for change in the world.

Different parts of the world have different religious customs. Thus, when war breaks out between different nations, the fighting is not only on the level of military skill. It is also a fight between the different life values of each religion. In some parts of the world, people value a peaceful personality; at least it is a spiritual standard. Not everybody does it, but still they accept it as a standard. In some other parts of the world, people honor the personality of a warlike hero type. By the different evolution within a region, which results in a certain religious expression, different values are held about life. Thus, the tendency or interest of each society is different. These differences are not easy to resolve, because they are the promotions of different religions.

If you wish to sit down to decide which side in an international conflict is right and which one is wrong, I think you can save yourself the trouble. It is not accurate. It cannot be judged except when an invasion is seen. Simply, you do not have enough time to review all the historical events to decide that. Emotion and hostility has usually built up for a long time regarding territory and rights.

So my expectation or wish to bring about a harmonious world is that people do not need to hold tightly onto any standpoint of racialism, nationalism, or particular religious background. A person cannot give up his race or background, but can be open to accepting others. This means no extreme clinging to one point of view.

This is my personal vision. To change to a new way of peace, we must keep old wounds and customs from being obstacles to the new generation of people. This is why I offer many books which talk about the same and different subjects. I am not the type of person to be involved in social movements, but I offer these ideas. Whoever among my young friends is interested in supporting my idea and wish to make it as your personal position, please write to the center in Atlanta. May all of you together bring about a new world.

My new order for the world is a different conception than the new order of any world political leader. My interest is not politics; my interest is to first let us have a spiritual breakthrough, and move through all the obstacles.

IX
The Subtle Truth

It appears among all things.
It will come to you by itself
at the time when you recognize it.
It is wrong to keep searching
everywhere.
You will learn that,
looking for it was just like looking for fire in ice.

Conclusion: What is Natural?

Q: Master Ni, what does natural mean? We all live with nature. What is the specific meaning, as Taoists talk about it?

Master Ni: In the wintertime, we walk into a field and see the vegetation in the surroundings. At that time of year, the plants mostly have become yellowish and dried up. Nature is the power, the magic power, which can return things to their green state and let them regain their life. This revival power of nature is the specific focus of the Taoist and is his confidence in life. We believe we never die. We always have a chance to be green, to be revitalized with natural support. The root of life, the soul of life and the seeds of life are our responsibility. We need to maintain ourselves, nurture, grow and become enduring as we engage in those external life experiences of which we are capable.

In the world, nothing is everlasting. From the surface of the physical level to the depth of nature, the root is Tao. To gain Tao means to reach the root. To learn Tao means to learn the subtle law. We operate our life in accordance and in coherence with the subtle law. This is the simple essence of the original Taoism. That is what I have learned, that is what I keep working on and what I promote to you. I make all other teachings and cultural achievements experiences of the immortal essence.

Q: Then, what is nature as Taoists think of it?

Master Ni: Nature itself is energy. The entire world is composed of formed energy and unformed energy, even space itself is energy; it is made up of different kinds of energy, that is all. Although conceptually we talk about fields of energy, capacities of energy and forms of energy, classifying and categorizing them as different matters, in reality the entirety of nature is one energy, it is one big life.

We are a small life. This is the basic understanding of the ancient developed ones.

So now we come to talk about where we live, the earth. The earth is also a kind of energy; it is an energy formation, a kind of amassed energy. We contact the earth every day. Sometimes we ignore its beauty. It is important to recognize the earth as a life with its own wisdom and its own virtuous fulfillment. You may be interested in knowing about the wisdom of the earth. When you see all the beautiful flowers in the trees and in the wilderness, that is the wisdom of the earth.

I believe you are widely read people. You have contacted many beautiful, creative minds, the great minds of the world, many philosophers and sages. Yes, they are wise, but I say reluctantly, all their wisdom can be compared to a tiny flower in a meadow. I am sorry to say that. We have to recognize that flowers are the wisdom of earth. How about fruit? Fruit, grains, beans and vegetables are the virtuous fulfillment of the earth. We rely on them. Without them, I do not know what kind of creatures we would become. Earth bestows its grace on us. How do we treat it? We view it as having no soul. It does not matter how we damage it. What fairness is there in this?

Look up at the sky. The sky is so big, it is enormous. Although it is enormous, it is energy; it is alive. Do you think that there is any wisdom to the sky? Let me tell you, we have to recognize that the sun, moon and stars are the wisdom of the sky. Without their light, we would still live in darkness, just like living in a big cave with no light source. The light emitted from the sun, moon and stars are the virtuous fulfillment of the sky. Thus, the sky bestows its grace on us.

The *Tao Teh Ching* says there are four great things: human beings, the earth, the sky and Tao, which is also called the subtle law. We have been talking about wisdom and virtuous fulfillment; those are positive and beautiful things that happen in the world and behind them there is the subtle law that manages them. The truly positive things in the world give only beauty and benefit, and are harmless. If anything is done with harmlessness, it is Heavenly energy.

The *Tao Teh Ching* also says that humans are supported and receive birth from the background of the subtle law of Tao. It is also called the subtle origin; in ancient times, they called it that. In his book Lao Tzu writes that people can conform with the virtue of the earth as the earth conforms with the virtue of the sky and the sky conforms with the virtue of the subtle law. We live on earth; does our life give forth flowers and bear fruit? By this I mean, does our life have virtuous fulfillment? If not, then the earth is still our teacher to have the virtuous fulfillment in our life and adopt nothing of these human discriminating concepts.

Some people think that because of our cultural development we humans are masters on earth but we are not; we still have something to learn from the earth. And surely we would like to learn from the sky. For these two basic things, wisdom and virtuous fulfillment, it does not matter if we learn them from the earth, the sky or the subtle law. The main thing is a sincere wish to learn from nature, because these three are aspects of nature.

All of this is important to understand. What is nature? Nature is not personal instinct or impulse. Many people think that if they follow their impulses that they are being natural, but that is shallow, individual nature, not spiritual development. If you follow impulse, you will not see the deep nature.

Now we come to the second layer of the reality of nature. In Chinese folk Taoism, originally the highest God was Yuan Shyy Tien Tsun, the subtle origin, or the Heavenly origin, or the origin of the highest spirituality. But, after a while, people did not feel that the energy connection was strong enough because it was too far from their lives, so they chose what they thought was a new and higher god to replace the old god. The new god was the Jade Emperor. Because the word "emperor" has the connotation of ruler, somebody who has power and the great interfering strength to cause trouble, they chose that word to describe this new god. But unfortunately, they did not truly understand what Jade Emperor means. By that, they had created a new god, they did not just replace the name of the god. Once they over-externalized spiritual reality, the meaning began to sink down. In reality, Jade Emperor means the spiritual energy within your life; that is, the true master of your life.

The western god is different; it is a creator. The Taoist god, the highest god, is the subtle origin; this means that everything must have an origin. All nature must grow up through a natural process. Everything can be traced back to the subtle origin. The subtle origin is unformed itself; it transcends the human conceptual function. Thus, everything has its form, but before it is formed, there is its unformed origin. This unformed origin is also what we call the universal mother or the mother of the universe. Sometimes we also use the Tai Chi diagram to describe it.

It is not that the reality of nature has changed; it is the human mind that has changed its conception. The reality of the highest god did not change; what changed was the conception of the highest god in the human mind. In Taoism, we believe that creative energy is the main energy of the highest god, it is godly energy. Only when initiating, or creative, energy is paired and accompanied with accomplishing energy can something be realized. This is why Creative Energy and Accomplishing Energy, Chyan and K'un, are the first two hexagrams of the *I Ching*, for it is these which initiate all the formations of change. The Chinese word for "accomplishing energy" can also be translated into English as "receptive energy." Why do we translate K'un as accomplishing energy? The ancient Chinese sages established their knowledge from life, they did not create an imaginary or ideological world. I would like to give an example of these energies taken from those times. If we observed a husband and wife, or man and woman who stayed together in those days, we would notice that the man went out to hunt and brought back an animal for their dinner. This is initiating energy. The woman, through the cooking process, makes it ready to be served. This is accomplishing energy. Today the hunting is a little different; it has the symbolic form of money, but basically the action is the same. So in any kind of community life, man and woman, leader and followers, and so forth, there must be an initiating energy and an accomplishing energy that work together to realize a thing. This is the nature of the world;

this illustrates the pattern of natural energy. One single energy cannot exist by itself. Nature is not the existence or dominance of creative energy alone.

Then there is also destructive energy. The purpose of destruction is to prepare for new creations. I can give you the example using my writing process: first I talk in public or at home on a tape and create a basic sketch of what I wish to say. The typist transcribes the tape and returns the first draft to me. After I make a better version or draft, the old one is destroyed or put aside. The old draft is not published. That shows how the new creative work is brought forth from the discarded or destroyed version. I would like to give another example. In our bodies, old cells die and new cells are born. Despite this constant process of birth and death within our very own bodies, the human being itself is healthy and whole.

Yin and yang arise always at the same time; there is no single performance, there is no sense of single dominance. Anyone who tells you that God means the dominance of one energy is not being accurate. We truly believe, that at specific times, nature tends to be creative or, at other times, that nature tends to be destructive. Harmony and balance is Godly energy; but in nature, we always see that creativity and destruction alternate and that one or the other extends more than its opposite at different times and occasions. This keeps the world moving further. This is called Tai Chi. Behind that alternation and movement is the subtle law. As to where nature itself comes from, we call that the subtle origin.

The third thing I would like to discuss with you is more practical. Some teachers, according to their own experience, organize a special program for spiritual achievement, such as "the hundred days of building the foundation" in the Taoist tradition. But prior to beginning that, much preparation is necessary. Nobody can jump suddenly into doing meditation for one or two hours. That is not a good idea; the practice needs to be built up, little by little.

So now you have become interested in doing spiritual cultivation. Because we are always attending to something and have a lot of movement in our regular lives, when we sit down to meditate we may find it difficult to keep still. Can we sit still in any given posture for three minutes? Three minutes is a good start; then build it up to five minutes. Then build up to twenty minutes, a half hour and so forth.

When people are young, they need to look for wisdom in life as their first priority and learn some Taoist arts such as T'ai Chi movement, the Eight Treasures and other valuable practices to maintain their general health and improve their internal condition. It is important to maintain yourself in good shape inside and out. Women over 40 and men over 50 need to be more serious spiritually, assuming they have reached some degree of financial stability. Women over 50 and men over 60 need to rely on external conditions which are hard to maintain, such as having a healthy body. They can start the preparation for spiritual life earlier. The skills, knowledge and opportunities for older people are more difficult; then cultivation comes as a remedy. It is better not to rely on external help such as medication when you are young but on your own knowledge of how to organize your life to lengthen your youthfulness.

If we are not careful when we are young, we will face the problem of becoming worn out in later years, after having extended ourselves in too many directions and thus exhausted ourselves. At such a time, many people go looking for a special formula to help them.

Among all the secret formulas of saving yourself spiritually, 99% are promises to help, but they are useless. There is only one real way to lengthen your years, to catch what was lost, in those remaining minutes. About that one true way, even if you find the right teacher to give you the correct knowledge, you still may not have the ability or be in a condition to utilize that special knowledge. Then your hopes will turn out to be an empty dream.

My earnest and truthful suggestion is to start now at whatever age you are. Chang An, the capitol of the Tang Dynasty, with all its high glamour, was not built in a day. Or as you say, "Rome was not built in a day." Remember also, no city is immortal. It is good to be serious and responsible about taking care of your precious life. Your life is your opportunity to evolve towards immortality.

Meditate to achieve your objectives and fulfill your goal. The purpose of meditation is not to numb your mind, it is for the gathering of your energy. That is the basic goal, so do the energy gathering. After a certain length of time, let us say 20 or 30 minutes, if you feel you have done it right, if you feel benefitted, you can then stop. Meditation is not a negative exercise to fossilize you or your vitality.

In the practice of real Taoism, we do not set up any rigid doctrines. Let us take the example of diet. People of different ages, professions and stages of cultivation need different diets. With knowledge of proper food and eating habits, people eat what their physical health really demands and continue to attain their physical and spiritual growth. At first, people eat to satisfy their taste buds. They continue to eat whatever they want until they attain some growth, when they discover that eating this way causes their stomachs to ache or they notice they become sluggish. At that time they naturally stop eating meat, overeating or eating too frequently because from inside themselves, they have learned to choose a good diet. They then eat according to their different ages, professions, and levels of spiritual cultivation. This is a matter of growth; this is called naturalness. It is not something somebody else establishes and forces you to do. In many different areas of life, there are some people who would rather let others choose or organize a program for them whereas, in reality, you need natural growth. Otherwise, you will come back to your old habits of eating unhealthy things or eating too much.

If I would stop my students from eating a big meal, they could try to please me or try to follow the requirement and do well. But once they were on their own, they would do whatever they liked because this kind of external requirement is not natural.

To follow Taoism is to follow the principle of naturalness, which brings us to the question: "Should you have sex or shouldn't you?" General organized religion says that if you do cultivation for spiritual achievement, you should not have sex. Now let us observe the people of those religions, can they meet that requirement? Can they tolerate that condition? Following such an injunction is not at all true achievement, it is complying with an external demand. True achievement is when, one day, you lose interest, not because you are sick but because your knowledge and awareness is growing. You are decreasing your sexual desire or you are choosing a different way of doing sex.

In the beginning, you are commanded by sexual desire, then, later, it is not at all the same. You are not commanded by sexual desire. You can have sex but if you do not have it, that is okay because you do not need it. If you have the right partner and you are correctly motivated, you respond, otherwise you do not. Achievement comes from naturalness. Growth comes from naturalness; it does not come from a typical human attitude of mind that organizes a thing, like the example I sometimes give of putting fruit in a can. That kind of process controls how many pieces there are and how sweet it is; all pre-organized. Growth is not like that.

So finally, we say, the conviction about life of the ancient achieved ones is so simple: God is creative and God is also destructive; the true God is a harmony of the two forces. If you insist that God is the creator, let God be the creator of harmony. Please do not let God be the creator of problems. By being that, he would make all spiritual and responsible people work on his incomplete sixth day creation: humans with a whole lot of problems. The stage of the God of problems should be over. Let the epoch of the God of harmony begin within and without all humans.

It was a natural custom for people to dedicate the first day as Heaven's day, the second day as earth's day and the third day to all human ancestors without discrimination, as human day. You might wonder what day we could use to dedicate to Tao. You may wonder why the subtle law, the subtle truth of nature, is not worthy of having a particular day dedicated to it. We need to dedicate all the days of our lives to it, not just one particular day. The way of dedication is to grow your own flowers and to have your own virtuous fulfillment as do the subtle origin, Heaven and Earth; then humans can work equally with these great three.

Learn from what Heaven, Earth and the subtle origin do. Shall we do things only for ourselves, and not also for others? That is the essence of the conviction about life held by the ancient developed ones. We are not taught by the ancient developed ones to participate in dogfights. We are taught to share whatever we have achieved with other people who can take support from it. You do this without our asking credit, seeking a title or expecting fellowship.

BOOKS IN ENGLISH BY MASTER NI

Harmony - The Art of Life - ***New Publication!***
Harmony occurs when two different things find the point at which they can link together. The point of linkage, if healthy and helpful, brings harmony. Harmony is a spiritual matter which relates to each individual's personal sensitivity and the sensitivity of each situation of daily life. Basically, harmony comes from understanding yourself. In this book, Master Ni shares some valuable Taoist understanding and insight about the ability to bring harmony within one's own self, one's relationships and the world. 208 pages, Stock No. BHARM, softcover, $14.95

Attune Your Body With Dao-In: Taoist Exercise for a Long and Happy Life - *New Publication!* - Dao-In is a series of typical Taoist movements which are traditionally used for physical energy conducting. These exercises were passed down from the ancient achieved Taoists and immortals. The ancients discovered that Dao-In exercises not only solved problems of stagnant energy, but also increased their health and lengthened their years. The exercises are also used as practical support for cultivation and the higher achievements of spiritual immortality. 144 pages, BDAOI Softcover with photographs, $14.95

The Key to Good Fortune: Refining Your Spirit - *New Publication!*
A translation of Straighten Your Way (Tai Shan Kan Yin Pien) and The Silent Way of Blessing (Yin Chia Wen), which are the main guidance for a mature and healthy life. This amplified version of the popular booklet called The Heavenly Way includes a new commentary section by Master Ni which discusses how spiritual improvement can become an integral part of one's life and how to realize a Heavenly life on earth. 144 pages. Stock No. BKEYT. Softcover, $12.95

Eternal Light - *New Publication!*
In this book, Master Ni presents the life and teachings of his father, Grandmaster Ni, Yo San, who was a spiritually achieved person, a Taoist healer and teacher, and a source of inspiration to Master Ni in his life. Here is an intimate look at the lifestyle of a spiritual family. Some of the deeper teachings and understandings of spirituality passed from father to son are clearly given and elucidated. This book is recommended for those committed to living a spiritual way of life and wishing for higher achievement. 208 pages Stock No. BETER Softcover, $14.95

Quest of Soul - *New Publication!*
In Quest of Soul, Master Ni addresses many subjects relevant to understanding one's own soul, such as the religious concept of saving the soul, how to improve the quality of the personal soul, the high spiritual achievement of free soul, what happens spiritually at death and the universal soul. He guides the reader into deeper knowledge

of oneself and inspires each individual to move forward to increase both one's own personal happiness and spiritual level. 152 pages. Stock No. BQUES Softcover, $11.95

Nurture Your Spirits - *New Publication!*
With truthful spiritual knowledge, you have better life attitudes that are more supportive to your existence. With truthful spiritual knowledge, nobody can cause you spiritual confusion. Where can you find such advantage? It would take a lifetime of development in a correct school, but such a school is not available. However, in this book, Master Ni breaks some spiritual prohibitions and presents the spiritual truth he has studied and proven. This truth may help you develop and nurture your own spirits which are the truthful internal foundation of your life being. Taoism is educational; its purpose is not to group people to build social strength but to help each individual build one's own spiritual strength. 176 pages. Stock No. BNURT Softcover, $12.95

Internal Growth Through Tao - *New Publication!*
Material goods can be passed from one person to another, but growth and awareness cannot be given in the same way. Spiritual development is related to one's own internal and external beingness. Through books, discussion or classes, wise people are able to use others' experiences to kindle their own inner light to help their own growth and live a life of no separation from their own spiritual nature. In this book, Master Ni teaches the more subtle, much deeper sphere of the reality of life that is above the shallow sphere of external achievement. He also shows the confusion caused by some spiritual teachings and guides you in the direction of developing spiritually by growing internally. 208 pages. Stock No. BINTE Softcover, $13.95

Power of Natural Healing - *New Publication!*
Master Ni discusses the natural capability of self-healing in this book, which is healing physical trouble untreated by medication or external measure. He offers information and practices which can assist any treatment method currently being used by someone seeking health. He goes deeper to discuss methods of Taoist cultivation which promote a healthy life, including Taoist spiritual achievement, which brings about health and longevity. This book is not only suitable for a person seeking to improve one's health condition. Those who wish to live long and happy, and to understand more about living a natural healthy lifestyle, may be supported by the practice of Taoist energy cultivation. 230 pages. Stock No. BPOWE Softcover, $14.95

Essence of Universal Spirituality
In this volume, as an open-minded learner and achieved teacher of universal spirituality, Master Ni examines and discusses all levels and topics of religious and spiritual teaching to help you develop your own correct knowledge of the essence existing above the differences in religious practice. He reviews religious teachings with hope to benefit modern people. This book is to help readers to come to understand

the ultimate truth and enjoy the achievement of all religions without becoming confused by them. 304 pages. Stock No. BESSE Softcover, $19.95

Guide to Inner Light

Modern life is controlled by city environments, cultural customs, religious teachings and politics that can all divert our attention away from our natural life being. As a result, we lose the perspective of viewing ourselves as natural completeness. This book reveals the development of ancient Taoist adepts. Drawing inspiration from their experience, modern people looking for the true source and meaning of life can find great teachings to direct and benefit them. The invaluable ancient Taoist development can teach us to reach the attainable spiritual truth and point the way to the Inner Light. Master Ni uses the ancient high accomplishments to make this book a useful resource. 192 pages. Stock No. BGUID. Softcover, $12.95

Stepping Stones for Spiritual Success

In Asia, the custom of foot binding was followed for close to a thousand years. In the West, people did not practice foot binding, but they bound their thoughts for a much longer period, some 1,500 to 1,700 years. Their mind and thinking became unnatural. Being unnatural expresses a state of confusion where people do not know what is right. Once they become natural again, they become clear and progress is great. Master Ni invites his readers to unbind their minds; in this volume, he has taken the best of the traditional teachings and put them into contemporary language to make them more relevant to our time, culture and lives. 160 pages. Stock No. BSTEP. Softcover, $12.95.

The Complete Works of Lao Tzu

Lao Tzu's Tao Teh Ching is one of the most widely translated and cherished works of literature in the world. It presents the core of Taoist philosophy. Lao Tzu's timeless wisdom provides a bridge to the subtle spiritual truth and practical guidelines for harmonious and peaceful living. Master Ni has included what is believed to be the only English translation of the Hua Hu Ching, a later work of Lao Tzu which has been lost to the general public for a thousand years. 212 pages. Stock No. BCOMP. Softcover, $12.95

Order The Complete Works of Lao Tzu and the companion Tao Teh Ching Cassette Tapes for only $23.00. Stock No. ABTAO.

The Book of Changes and the Unchanging Truth

The first edition of this book was widely appreciated by its readers, who drew great spiritual benefit from it. They found the principles of the I Ching to be clearly explained and useful to their lives, especially the helpful commentaries. The legendary classic I Ching is recognized as mankind's first written book of wisdom. Leaders and sages throughout history have consulted it as a trusted advisor which reveals the appropriate action to be taken in any of life's circumstances. This volume also includes over 200 pages of background material on Taoist principles of natural energy cycles, instruction and commentaries. New, revised second edition, 669 pages. Stock No. BBOOK. Hardcover, $35.50

The Story of Two Kingdoms

This volume is the metaphoric tale of the conflict between the Kingdoms of Light and Darkness. Through this unique story, Master Ni transmits the esoteric teachings of Taoism which have been carefully guarded secrets for over 5,000 years. This book is for those who are serious in their search and have devoted their lives to achieving high spiritual goals. 122 pages. Stock No. BSTOR. Hardcover, $14.50

The Way of Integral Life

This book can help build a bridge for those wishing to connect spiritual and intellectual development. It is most helpful for modern educated people. It includes practical and applicable suggestions for daily life, philosophical thought, esoteric insight and guidelines for those aspiring to give help and service to the world. This book helps you learn the wisdom of the ancient sages' achievement to assist the growth of your own wisdom and integrate it as your own new light and principles for balanced, reasonable living in worldly life. 320 pages. Softcover, $14.00, Stock No. BWAYS. Hardcover, $20.00, Stock No. BWAYH

Enlightenment: Mother of Spiritual Independence

The inspiring story and teachings of Master Hui Neng, the father of Zen Buddhism and Sixth Patriarch of the Buddhist tradition, highlight this volume. Hui Neng was a person of ordinary birth, intellectually unsophisticated, who achieved himself to become a spiritual leader. Master Ni includes enlivening commentaries and explanations of the principles outlined by this spiritual revolutionary. Having received the same training as all Zen Masters as one aspect of his training and spiritual achievement, Master Ni offers this teaching so that his readers may be guided in their process of spiritual development. 264 pages. Softcover, $12.50, Stock No. BENLS. Hardcover, $22.00, Stock No. BENLH

Attaining Unlimited Life

The thought-provoking teachings of Chuang Tzu are presented in this volume. He was perhaps the greatest philosopher and master of Taoism and he laid the foundation for the Taoist school of thought. Without his work, people of later generations would hardly recognize the value of Lao Tzu's teaching in practical, everyday life. He touches the organic nature of human life more deeply and directly than that of other great teachers. This volume also includes questions by students and answers by Master Ni. 467 pages. Softcover, $18.00, Stock No. BATTS; Hardcover, $25.00, Stock No. BATTH

The Gentle Path of Spiritual Progress

This book offers a glimpse into the dialogues of a Taoist master and his students. In a relaxed, open manner, Master Ni, Hua-Ching explains to his students the fundamental practices that are the keys to experiencing enlightenment in everyday life. Many of the traditional secrets of Taoist training are revealed. His students also ask a surprising range of questions, and Master Ni's answers touch on contemporary psychology, finances, sexual advice, how to use the I Ching as well as the telling of some fascinating Taoist legends. Softcover, $12.95, Stock No. BGENT

Spiritual Messages from a Buffalo Rider, A Man of Tao

This is another important collection of Master Ni's service in his worldly trip, originally published as one half of The Gentle Path. He had the opportunity to meet people and answer their questions to help them gain the spiritual awareness that we live at the command of our animal nature. Our buffalo nature rides on us, whereas an achieved person rides the buffalo. In this book, Master Ni gives much helpful knowledge to those who are interested in improving their lives and deepening their cultivation so they too can develop beyond their mundane beings. Softcover, $12.95, Stock No. BSPIR

8,000 Years of Wisdom, Volume I and II

This two volume set contains a wealth of practical, down-to-earth advice given by Master Ni to his students over a five year period, 1979 to 1983. Drawing on his training in Traditional Chinese Medicine, Herbology, Acupuncture and other Taoist arts, Master Ni gives candid answers to students' questions on many topics ranging from dietary guidance to sex and pregnancy, meditation techniques and natural cures for common illnesses. Volume I includes dietary guidance; 236 pages; Stock No. BWIS1 Volume II includes sex and pregnancy guidance; 241 pages; Stock No. BWIS2. Softcover, Each Volume $12.50

The Uncharted Voyage Towards the Subtle Light

Spiritual life in the world today has become a confusing mixture of dying traditions and radical novelties. People who earnestly and sincerely seek something more than just a way to fit into the complexities of a modern structure that does not support true self-development often find themselves spiritually struggling. This book provides a profound understanding and insight into the underlying heart of all paths of spiritual growth, the subtle origin and the eternal truth of one universal life. 424 pages. Stock No. BUNCH. Softcover, $14.50

The Heavenly Way

A translation of the classic Tai Shan Kan Yin Pien (Straighten Your Way) and Yin Chia Wen (The Silent Way of Blessing). The treaties in this booklet are the main guidance for a mature and healthy life. The purpose of this booklet is to promote the recognition of truth, because only truth can teach the perpetual Heavenly Way by which one reconnects oneself with the divine nature. 41 pages. Stock No. BHEAV. Softcover, $2.50

Footsteps of the Mystical Child
This book poses and answers such questions as: What is a soul? What is wisdom? What is spiritual evolution? The answers to these and many other questions enable readers to open themselves to new realms of understanding and personal growth. There are also many true examples about people's internal and external struggles on the path of self-development and spiritual evolution. 166 pages. Stock No. BFOOT. Softcover, $9.50

Workbook for Spiritual Development
This book offers a practical, down-to-earth, hands-on approach for those who are devoted to the path of spiritual achievement. The reader will find diagrams showing fundamental hand positions to increase and channel one's spiritual energy, postures for sitting, standing and sleeping cultivation as well as postures for many Taoist invocations. The material in this workbook is drawn from the traditional teachings of Taoism and summarizes thousands of years of little known practices for spiritual development. An entire section is devoted to ancient invocations, another on natural celibacy and another on postures. In addition, Master Ni explains the basic attitudes and understandings that are the foundation for Taoist practices. 224 pages. Stock No. BWORK. Softcover, $12.95

Poster of Master Lu
Color poster of Master Lu, Tung Ping (shown on cover of workbook), for use with the workbook or in one's shrine. 16" x 22"; Stock No. PMLTP. $10.95

Order the Workbook for Spiritual Development *and the companion Poster of Master Lu for $18.95.* Stock No. BPWOR.

The Taoist Inner View of the Universe
This presentation of Taoist metaphysics provides guidance for one's own personal life transformation. Master Ni has given all the opportunity to know the vast achievement of the ancient unspoiled mind and its transpiercing vision. This book offers a glimpse of the inner world and immortal realm known to achieved Taoists and makes it understandable for students aspiring to a more complete life. 218 pages. Stock No. BTAOI. Softcover, $14.95

Tao, the Subtle Universal Law
Most people are unaware that their thoughts and behavior evoke responses from the invisible net of universal energy. The real meaning of Taoist self-discipline is to harmonize with universal law. To lead a good stable life is to be aware of the actual conjoining of the universal subtle law with every moment of our lives. This book presents the wisdom and practical methods that the ancient Chinese have successfully used for centuries to accomplish this. 165 pages. Stock No. TAOS. Softcover, $7.50

MATERIALS ON TAOIST HEALTH, ARTS AND SCIENCES

BOOKS

The Tao of Nutrition by Maoshing Ni, Ph.D., with Cathy McNease, B.S., M.H. - Working from ancient Chinese medical classics and contemporary research, Dr. Maoshing Ni and Cathy McNease have compiled an indispensable guide to natural healing. This exceptional book shows the reader how to take control of one's health through one's eating habits. This volume contains 3 major sections: the first section deals with theories of Chinese nutrition and philosophy; the second describes over 100 common foods in detail, listing their energetic properties, therapeutic actions and individual remedies. The third section lists nutritional remedies for many common ailments. This book presents both a healing system and a disease prevention system which is flexible in adapting to every individual's needs. 214 pages. Stock No. BNUTR. Softcover, $14.50

Chinese Vegetarian Delights by Lily Chuang
An extraordinary collection of recipes based on principles of traditional Chinese nutrition. Many recipes are therapeutically prepared with herbs. Diet has long been recognized as a key factor in health and longevity. For those who require restricted diets and those who choose an optimal diet, this cookbook is a rare treasure. Meat, sugar, diary products and fried foods are excluded. Produce, grains, tofu, eggs and seaweeds are imaginatively prepared. 104 pages. Stock No. BCHIV. Softcover, $7.50

Chinese Herbology Made Easy - by Maoshing Ni, Ph.D.
This text provides an overview of Oriental medical theory, in-depth descriptions of each herb category, with over 300 black and white photographs, extensive tables of individual herbs for easy reference, and an index of pharmaceutical and Pin-Yin names. The distillation of overwhelming material into essential elements enables one to focus efficiently and develop a clear understanding of Chinese herbology. This book is especially helpful for those studying for their California Acupuncture License. 202 pages. Stock No. BCHIH. Softcover, 14.50

Crane Style Chi Gong Book - By Daoshing Ni, Ph.D.
Chi Gong is a set of meditative exercises that was developed several thousand years ago by Taoists in China. It is now practiced for healing purposes, combining breathing techniques, body movements and mental imagery to guide the smooth flow of energy throughout the body. This book gives a more detailed account and study of Chi Gong than the videotape alone. It may be used with or without the videotape. Includes complete instructions and information on using Chi Gong exercise as a medical therapy. 55 pages. Stock No. BCRAN. Spiral bound $10.50

VIDEO TAPES

Physical Movement for Spiritual Learning: Dao-In Physical Art for a Long and Happy Life (VHS) - by Master Ni. Dao-In is a series of typical Taoist movements which are traditionally used for physical energy conducting. These exercises were passed down from the ancient achieved Taoists and immortals. The ancients discovered that Dao-In exercises not only solved problems of stagnant energy, but also increased their health and lengthened their years. The exercises are also used as practical support for cultivation and the higher achievements of spiritual immortality. Master Ni, Hua-Ching, heir to the tradition of the achieved masters, is the first one who releases this important Taoist practice to the modern world in this 1 hour videotape. VHS $59.95

T'ai Chi Chuan: An Appreciation (VHS) - by Master Ni
Different styles of T'ai Chi Ch'uan as Movement have different purposes and accomplish different results. In this long awaited videotape, Master Ni, Hua-Ching presents three styles of T'ai Chi Movement handed down to him through generations of highly developed masters. They are the "Gentle Path," "Sky Journey," and "Infinite Expansion" styles of T'ai Chi Movement. The three styles are presented uninterrupted in this unique videotape and are set to music for observation and appreciation. VHS 30 minutes $49.95

Crane Style Chi Gong (VHS) - by Dr. Daoshing Ni, Ph.D.
Chi Gong is a set of meditative exercises developed several thousand years ago by ancient Taoists in China. It is now practiced for healing stubborn chronic diseases, strengthening the body to prevent disease and as a tool for further spiritual enlightenment. It combines breathing techniques, simple body movements, and mental imagery to guide the smooth flow of energy throughout the body. Chi gong is easy to learn for all ages. Correct and persistent practice will increase one's energy, relieve stress or tension, improve concentration and clarity, release emotional stress and restore general well-being. 2 hours Stock No. VCRAN. $65.95

Eight Treasures (VHS) - By Maoshing Ni, Ph.D.
These exercises help open blocks in a person's energy flow and strengthen one's vitality. It is a complete exercise combining physical stretching and toning and energy conducting movements coordinated with breathing. The Eight Treasures are an exercise unique to the Ni family. Patterned from nature, its 32 movements are an excellent foundation for Tai Chi Chuan or martial arts. 1 hour, 45 minutes. Stock No. VEIGH. $49.95

Tai Chi Chuan I & II (VHS) - By Maoshing Ni, Ph.D.
This exercise integrates the flow of physical movement with that of integral energy in the Taoist style of "Harmony," similar to the long form of Yang-style Tai Chi Chuan. Tai Chi has been practiced for thousands of years to help both physical longevity and spiritual cultivation. 1 hour each. Each Video Tape $49.95. Order both for $90.00. Stock Nos: Part I, VTAI1; Part II, VTAI2; Set of two, VTAI3.

AUDIO CASSETTES

Invocations: Health and Longevity and Healing a Broken Heart - By Maoshing Ni, Ph.D. This audio cassette guides the listener through a series of ancient invocations to channel and conduct one's own healing energy and vital force. "Thinking is louder than thunder." The mystical power by which all miracles are brought about is your sincere practice of this principle. 30 minutes. Stock No. AINVO. $8.95

Chi Gong for Stress Release - By Maoshing Ni, Ph.D.
This audio cassette guides you through simple, ancient breathing exercises that enable you to release day-to-day stress and tension that are such a common cause of illness today. 30 minutes. Stock No. ACHIS. $8.95

Chi Gong for Pain Management - By Maoshing Ni, Ph.D.
Using easy visualization and deep-breathing techniques that have been developed over thousands of years, this audio cassette offers methods for overcoming pain by invigorating your energy flow and unblocking obstructions that cause pain. 30 minutes. Stock No. ACHIP. $8.95

Tao Teh Ching Cassette Tapes
This classic work of Lao Tzu has been recorded in this two-cassette set that is a companion to the book translated by Master Ni. Professionally recorded and read by Robert Rudelson. 120 minutes. Stock No. ATAOT. $15.95

Order Master Ni's book, The Complete Works of Lao Tzu, and Tao Teh Ching Cassette Tapes for only $25.00. Stock No. ABTAO.

How To Order

Name: ______________________________

Address: ______________________________

City: ______________ *State:* ________ *Zip:* ________

Phone - Daytime: ______________ *Evening:* ______________

(We may telephone you if we have questions about your order.)

Qty.	Stock No.	Title/Description	Price Each	Total Price

Total amount for items ordered______________

Sales tax (CA residents only, 8-1/4%)______________

Shipping Charge (See below)______________

Total Amount Enclosed______________

Visa _____ *Mastercard* _____ *Expiration Date* ______________

Card number: ______________________________

Signature: ______________________________

Shipping: In the US, we use UPS when possible. Please give full street address or nearest crossroads. All packages are insured at no extra charge. If shipping to more than one address, use separate shipping charges. Remember: 1 - 10 copies of Heavenly Way, Tao Teh Ching audio tapes and each book and tape are single items. Posters (up to 5 per tube) are a separate item. Please allow 2 - 4 weeks for US delivery and 6 - 10 weeks for foreign surface mail.

By Mail: Complete this form with payment (US funds only, No Foreign Postal Money Orders, please) and mail to: Union of Tao and Man, 117 Stonehaven Way, Los Angeles, CA 90049

Phone Orders: (213) 472-9970 - You may leave credit card orders anytime on our answering machine. Please speak clearly and remember to leave your full name and daytime phone number. We will call only if we have a question with your order, there is a delay or you specifically ask for phone confirmation.

Inquiries: If you have questions concerning your order, please refer to the date and invoice number on the top center of your invoice to help us locate your order swiftly.

Shipping Charges -

- *Domestic Surface: First item $3.25, each additional, add $.50.*
- *Canada Surface: First item $3.25, each additional, add $1.00.*
- *Canada Air: First item $4.00, each additional, add $2.00*
- *Foreign Surface: First Item $3.50, each additional, add $2.00.*
- *Foreign Air: First item $12.00, each additional, add $7.00.*

For the Trade: Wholesale orders may be placed direct to publisher, or with NewLeaf, BookPeople, The Distributors, Inland Books, GreatWay in US or DeepBooks in Europe.

Thank you for your order

Spiritual Study Through the College of Tao

The College of Tao and the Union of Tao and Man were established formally in California in the 1970's. This tradition is a very old spiritual culture of mankind, holding long experience of human spiritual growth. Its central goal is to offer healthy spiritual education to all people of our society. This time tested tradition values the spiritual development of each individual self and passes down its guidance and experience.

Master Ni carries his tradition from its country of origin to the west. He chooses to avoid making the mistake of old-style religions that have rigid establishments which resulted in fossilizing the delicacy of spiritual reality. Rather, he prefers to guide the teachings of his tradition as a school of no boundary rather than a religion with rigidity. Thus, the branches or centers of this Taoist school offer different programs of similar purpose. Each center extends its independent service, but all are unified in adopting Master Ni's work as the foundation of teaching to fulfill the mission of providing spiritual education to all people.

The centers offer their classes, teaching, guidance and practices on building the groundwork for cultivating a spiritually centered and well-balanced life. As a person obtains the correct knowledge with which to properly guide himself or herself, he or she can then become more skillful in handling the experiences of daily life. The assimilation of good guidance in one's practical life brings about different stages of spiritual development.

Any interested individual is welcome to join and learn to grow for oneself. You might like to join the center near where you live, or you yourself may be interested in organizing a center or study group based on the model of existing centers. In that way, we all work together for the spiritual benefit of all people. We do not require any religious type of commitment.

The learning is life. The development is yours. The connection of study may be helpful, useful and serviceable, directly to you.

- -

Mail to: Union of Tao and Man, 117 Stonehaven Way, Los Angeles, CA 90049

____ I wish to be put on the mailing list of the Union of Tao and Man to be notified of classes, educational activities and new publications.

Name:____

Address:____

City:_____________________________State:___________Zip:______

Herbs Used by Ancient Taoist Masters

The pursuit of everlasting youth or immortality throughout human history is an innate human desire. Long ago, Chinese esoteric Taoists went to the high mountains to contemplated nature, strengthen their bodies, empower their minds and develop their spirit. From their studies and cultivation, they gave China alchemy and chemistry, herbology and acupuncture, the I Ching, astrology, martial arts and T'ai Chi Chuan, Chi Gong and many other useful kinds of knowledge.

Most important, they handed down in secrecy methods for attaining longevity and spiritual immortality. There were different levels of approach; one was to use a collection of food herb formulas that were only available to highly achieved Taoist masters. They used these food herbs to increase energy and heighten vitality. This treasured collection of herbal formulas remained within the Ni family for centuries.

Now, through Traditions of Tao, the Ni family makes these foods available for you to use to assist the foundation of your own positive development. It is only with a strong foundation that expected results are produced from diligent cultivation.

As a further benefit, in concert with the Taoist principle of self-sufficiency, Traditions of Tao offers the food herbs along with the Union of Tao and Man's publications in a distribution opportunity for anyone serious about financial independence.

Send to: *Traditions of Tao*
117 Stonehaven Way
Los Angeles, CA 90049

☐ *Please send me a Traditions of Tao brochure.*

☐ *Please send me information on becoming an independent distributor of Traditions of Tao herbal products and publications.*

Name ______________________________

Address ______________________________

City ______________ *State* ________ *Zip* ________

Phone (day) ______________ *(night)* ______________

Index of Some Topics